TO
LIVE
GOD'S
WORD

TO
LIVE
GOD'S
WORD

by

Yvonne Goulet

Photographs by Todd Brennan

THE THOMAS MORE PRESS

Chicago, Illinois

ISBN o.88347-104-3

The author and publisher wish to acknowledge with thanks permission
to print quotations from the following:

ALL THE KING'S MEN by James Ruoff from TWENTIETH CENTURY
LITERATURE. Copyright 1957 by Twentieth Century Literature,
Hofstra University.

ALL THE KING'S MEN by Robert Penn Warren. Copyright © 1946 by
Robert Penn Warren. Used by permission Harcourt Brace Jovanovich,
Inc.

"Anecdote of a Jar" by Wallace Stevens from THE COLLECTED
POEMS OF WALLACE STEVENS. Copyright 1954 by Wallace Stevens.
By permission of Alfred A. Knopf.

THE AUTOBIOGRAPHY OF WILLIAM CARLOS WILLIAMS. Copyright
1951 by William Carlos Williams. Reprinted by permission of New
Directions.

"The Body and Liturgy" by David Loomis from LITURGY by David
Loomis. Copyright by The Liturgical Conference, Inc., 810 Rhode
Island Ave., N.E., Washington, D.C. 20018.

Contents

To Live God's Word

Introduction
THE TASK OF THE CHRISTIAN

> A word is dead
> When it is said
> Some say.
> I say it just
> Begins to live
> That day.
>
> Emily Dickinson

THIS is a book about Incarnation, about the Word having become flesh and dwelt among us. But, more to the point, it is a book about incarnation with a small i, about how the Word only begins to live in us when it is said, and how saying the word means living it.

It is largely a book of reflections on my own experience, struggling to live the Gospel in the concrete, limited circumstances of my own life, and failing miserably.

But the Christ life is one of hope. The Gospel is a goad. For those who believe, it cannot be ignored or escaped. Like Francis Thompson's "Hound of Heaven," the Lord is always in pursuit, assuring his people that they are loved, and needed.

Christian life is, I think, essentially an attempt to live in the tension set up between the sublime model and ideals that Jesus presented in Scripture, and the events of our lives. The Gospel becomes a standard by which we measure (but do not judge) ourselves, others, our families, communities, parishes, society as a whole, the Church.

The Gospel is insistent. It cannot be remade. It must be made one's own. Jesus must become not just the Lord but *my* Lord. And the Word must live in my personal, particular circumstances.

In the Public Television series *The Long Search*,

To Live God's Word

Ronald Eyre tried each week in forty-five minutes or so, to come to an understanding of one of the world's great religions. In the program on Catholicism, called "Rome, Leeds, and the Desert," he succeeded superbly. Incarnation, the Church as "the Body of God," was the point made insistently by all of the participants, however subtly. A Spanish priest, for example, spoke with Eyre about the motives of the pilgrims who visit the Shrine of Montserrat. "Spiritual feelings, faith, is a grace, a gift of God. It's always incarnated into life." He neatly did away with all of Eyre's attempts to have him theorize. "Prayer doesn't exist. The only reality is men and women, and children and young people who pray."

In this same sense, then, the Church doesn't exist in the abstract, but in the individual persons who give the Lord access to their own time through their bodies. For the Lord came in a particular time and place. To come in our time and place, he requires our cooperation. He becomes present only if he can use our hands, heads, feet.

All of creation below man, is will-less and therefore utterly docile. God can inhabit matter because it surrenders utterly to him. All of lower creation allows the power and glory of God to penetrate. It is both man's glory and his shame that man is free, has a will, can resist God.

This point was made beautifully in the play *A Man for All Seasons* by Robert Bolt. In it, Thomas More, who himself is a model of incarnation, speaks to his daughter Margaret about man's uniqueness in creation: "God made the angels to show him splendor, as he made the animals for innocence, and plants for their simplicity. But man he made to serve him wittingly, in the tangle of his mind."

"Tangle" seems a perfect word choice for a description of the human mind. Choices are seldom clear, even with the Gospel's guidance. And becoming an adult Christian requires a person to struggle with the Lord, to wrestle with the Scriptures. Consciousness comes only through effort and much backsliding. The Kingdom, after all, is still embryonic in each of us, and while the tide of salvation history carries us forward, and while God's will is inexorably fulfilled, each person must decide whether to resist or go with that tide. And each person starts from the beginning. Each of us, in his or her faith life, recapitulates the progress of the Christian church from its beginning.

Entering consciously into salvation history means making the will a gift to God. It is a gift we withhold, and yet it is the one demanded if the Lord is to be Lord in our lives. It is the hardest gift to give, but without it, we wrestle continually with the angels on inadequacy, doubt, fear.

Getting by giving is the paradox of the Gospel. As T.S. Eliot said,

Yvonne Goulet

"We only exist, only suspire
Consumed by either fire or fire."

The giving that is required of a Christian is total. It costs, again according to Eliot, "not less than everything" and the cost is too much for most of us, most of the time. William F. Lynch in his classic work of literary criticism *Christ and Apollo*, demonstrates this point superbly. He speaks of Albert Camus' novel *The Fall*, in which a man hears a woman plunge into the river and fails to turn back to help. He is haunted the rest of his life by that moment, and his refusal to act.

Father Lynch comments: ". . . There is no easy way to beauty. The water would be so cold! It is no joke, nor a dream, this thing called beauty. We can jump into the desert in a moment, but the way of the literal is longer, and there are no shortcuts through or around it."

This is no indictment of the contemplative vocation, but it does suggest that, like Jesus, we go into the desert to gather strength for service. The praise and worship of God are best accomplished, Jesus demonstrated for us, in serving other people.

Do Christians believe the words of Jesus: "Whatsoever you do to the least of my brothers, that you do to me." Do we really see the suffering Lord, the crucified Christ in those who suffer, and in ourselves when we suffer? When we serve a person in need, is it truly Christ we serve?

Why is radical charity so rare that someone like Mother Teresa of Calcutta becomes a celebrity? We perhaps need radical models of such charity, of people who give totally, to teach us that we can give some.

Why have we Catholics failed to be, like Mother Teresa, models of radical charity and of justice to the world? Why cannot the world see in the Church, individually and collectively, the suffering servant of others?

Yvonne Goulet

Because, Dietrich Bonhoeffer suggests in *The Cost of Discipleship*, we have opted for cheap rather than costly grace. "Such grace is costly because it calls us to follow, and it is grace because it calls us to follow Jesus Christ. It is costly because it costs a man his life and it is grace because it gives a man the only true life. It is costly because it condemns sin, and grace because it justifies the sinner. Above all, it is costly because it cost God the life of his Son: 'Ye were bought at a price,' and what has cost God much cannot be cheap for us. Above all, it is grace because God did not reckon his Son too dear a price to pay for our life, but delivered him up for us. Costly grace is the Incarnation of God."

And for us, costly grace is allowing God to become incarnate in us. If we do, we can expect the cross, but we cannot also expect resurrection. It is surrendering our natural gifts to the breath of the spirit, the inspiration of grace.

Such surrender lets our hearts of stone become

hearts of flesh. This is incarnation too, in which we turn our natural human sensibilities to the workings of grace.

But grace builds on nature and where the natural gifts are not discovered and cultivated, the grace of God cannot work. We fail, then, on the plane of nature, and our first failure is that of the senses—seeing, hearing. Many times priests have told me that such and such a problem does not exist in his parish, that there is no marital discord, hunger, discrimination. Of course there are such things, but we do not cultivate our perception.

A woman was in the process of getting a divorce when her parish priest visited her home a few years ago. After a pleasant visit, he got up to leave, saying, "Well, I guess everything is fine here." The woman, flabbergasted, said, "Father, my husband and I are getting a divorce." When they sat down again, the real communication began. But how many people are too inarticulate or too fearful to say the truths about themselves? And how few of us look or listen carefully enough to see and hear the truth that is not said?

And why do we fail to see and hear? Have we built walls around ourselves, defense mechanisms to protect us from too much pain? Or have we been deadened by life, lost the sense of wonder, the ability to respond? If we cannot wonder at the brilliance of the fall sky or the intricacy of an aphid, we may have simply buried our sensuous nature, or had it buried.

Most of us are victims of an educational system which rewards conformity rather than freshness of vision. In conforming to the process, we tend to lose the sharpness of sense that characterized us as young children.

We also fail simply to pay attention. We tend to be so preoccupied with the inner workings of our lives, or so distracted by external activities, that we rarely look at things or people.

To Live God's Word

The power of the senses is recoverable, though. It takes practice, first paying attention to the physical world, to perceive the loveliness that exists even in decay. Incarnation, letting the Lord live in us, requires then, first of all, that we hear the cry in the night.

The second failure, I think, is that of compassion. It is essentially a failure of imagination and is directly related to the failure in sensation described above. Many people are terribly sensitive to matters concerning themselves, but totally lack the ability to feel with or for another.

We cannot identify with the situation of another probably because we cannot imagine his circumstances. And often, we cannot imagine, because our education has not rewarded the exercise of creative thinking. Religious education, I think, should involve the liberation of the imagination. The quest for the holy, it has been said, is exactly the same as the quest for the beautiful. Imagination allows us to project experiences of pain, bereavement, loneliness, onto others.

But as a flaccid muscle has no strength, an unexercised imagination cannot feel with others. The arts, I think, are the remedy. They exercise the imagination, both in the process of creating and appreciating. An atrophied imagination can be made healthy through this kind of exercise, and the exposure to beauty will be seen to lead to goodness as well.

A third possible failure is that of generosity. Bonhoeffer tells us grace costs. The water is so cold. It is far easier to flee into the desert than to plunge into the cold water. (And, perhaps, it is easier to find God in the desert than it is to see him in other people.) Incarnation is often uncomfortable. And it may be this, more than anything else, that keeps people from acting.

It is clear that work without prayer is incomplete, but faith without works, as the Epistle of James tells us, is dead.

"If one of the brothers or one of the sisters is in need of clothes and has not enough food to live on and one of you says to him, 'I wish you well; keep yourself warm and eat plenty,' without giving him these bare necessities of life, then what good is that? Faith is like that: if good works do not go with it, it is quite dead."

It is possible to see the task of preaching the Gospel as a largely vocal undertaking. And it is possible to see our task as Christians primarily as praising God. But the Lord told us that it is mercy and not sacrifice that he yearns for. It is quite encouraging to note that both the evangelicals, who have, in the past, stressed preaching, and the charismatics, who have emphasized praising, have now begun to develop solid social consciences. Praise the Lord!

A final failure in the lack of response to the sounds from the water is fear—the failure of courage. Perhaps that is the easiest problem to remedy. If one has acquired the ability to see, to feel with, and to be motivated to act, it seems just a short step to conquering one's fear of acting. But, still, lack of self esteem, hesitancy, fear, hold back many.

We need to encourage one another, especially in this area. Dorothy Day said, "We are all corrupted every day. We hold each other up by prayer." A situation may require a simple act of charity. It may call for putting into action the principles of justice. We need to begin to act and to encourage others to act.

It would be well, in such circumstances, to reflect on the uniqueness of each person, the gifts that each person has for the mission of his or her life. It would be well to meditate on why the Lord has placed us in these particular circumstances. If faith means anything, it is that God's plan for us is revealed through the events and circumstances of our lives, and part of these are the demands made upon us. We should reflect that, since our gifts and situations are unique, it is imperative that we act if God's plan is to fructify.

To Live God's Word

And we must come to know that, just as it is in this place that the Lord wants me to act, so it is at this time. Procrastination means a slowing of the coming of the Kingdom. He wants me to respond to these circumstances. This does not obviate long range planning, of course, but it does mean the ability to see present needs as well as anticipate future needs.

To respond effectively to a situation in the here and now requires another quality, however, one which to some extent is the result of the aforementioned factors (sensitivity, compassion, generosity, courage). That quality is spontaneity, the ability to act appropriately on the spur of the moment. It is total response to the unique set of circumstances we find ourselves in. It means being loose enough to get out of programmed, rigid, prepatterned modes of behavior. It may be the quality most lacking in Catholic Christians.

It is the power of the Holy Spirit that allows us to do the right thing (say the right thing) instantaneously. But grace builds on nature, and the Spirit cannot use a rigid instrument.

Spontaneity takes into account the news as well as the needs. It is attuned to "the teachable moment." It does not deal in abstractions but teaches faith, for example, in the life circumstances of the person being taught.

Spontaneity is never tempted to solve the problems of Bangladesh while overlooking those of the neighborhood (though it may try to do both). It never misses an opportunity to enflesh principle with example. It bridges the gap between the ideals of the Gospel and the real world. Without it, we tend to respond to yesterday's needs with yesterday's answers. Incarnation means an absorption primarily in the time and place where the Lord is touching us. It is making this time, this place, open to God's grace and power through our own gifts.

The task of every Christian, in my opinion, then, is to make sense out of the circumstances of his/her life in Christian terms, to find the common theme which runs through his experiences, the center of his life, and to do this unselfconsciously, allowing the Lord to increase his power in one's life as the ego diminishes.

Following, then, is one person's view of how the Gospel enfleshes life, one account of a person trying to live the word.

Part I

PRAYING

Yvonne Goulet

WORSHIP

"Every thing that is, is holy now."
John L'Heureux, "A Solemne Musicke"

INCARNATION means transforming the Word into one's own flesh. The process is a struggle because we yearn for expansion, for adventure. We seek to conquer space, whereas our true mission is to conquer time, the little time given us between birth and death.

Ultimately, the quest for adventure must be replaced with the quest for depth, for understanding our experiences instead of ever looking for new experiences. There is a difference between knowing everything and knowing ourselves very well.

Contemplation, then, is an essential part of incarnation. It is finding the God of the universe in our hearts, in our breath, in our own impulses.

Real prayer results in a sense of being inhabited.

To Live God's Word

The process is sometimes referred to as centering, or of finding a center. It is a remedy for the alienation people feel, the fragmentation we experience as a result of the endless assault on our senses of the world and of the media. (Sometimes I think the three great distractions are the World, the Media, the Devil.)

Prayer results in a sense of ourselves as situated, as rooted, as at peace.

In view of the doctrine of Incarnation, it seems ironic that it is eastern rather than western spirituality that takes into consideration the body.

Now, the Church, in theory, is immensely incarnational. The community, the visible church is the rooting of oneself in a people as surely as the Hebrews were rooted. Similarly, the heart of Catholic worship is the Eucharist, the sign of Christ's presence among us, and the cause of the unity among us.

But in spite of this body-consciousness on a

theoretical level, the western Church, western spirituality, takes little notice of bodies.

In eastern spirituality, there is far more awareness of the total human person. The discipline of yoga, for example, requires certain postures, attention to one's breath. The flow of energy and of blood must not be impeded if the human spirit is to be at peace. Yoga sees the physical as one with the spiritual, whereas western spirituality leaps into the infinite.

While in recent years liturgical renewal has brought about greater signs of attention to the present realities (intercessory prayers, the rite of peace), nevertheless, it seems there is insufficient attention generally of celebrant and congregation to the "now" in which the salvific event is being reenacted.

Although Christianity is the great plunge into reality, the liturgy, for many reasons, for many years, was an escape from reality into the infinite.

To Live God's Word

The Roman Catholic liturgy is still largely worship of the head rather than of the total person. Consider the comments by David Loomis in an article in *Liturgy* entitled, "The Body and Liturgy:"

> We who call ourselves Christian proclaim the triumphant message that the word was made flesh, that God has overcome the alienation between himself and the everyday world, that all of life (even the most carnal) can participate in God's forgiving and fulfilling love. And yet in our worship (prayer) we largely reverse the intent of the incarnation. Everything becomes abstracted. In our worship, flesh becomes words rather than the word being made flesh. Rather than the passion, the eros with which Jesus related to God, the Church normally worships as if God were an impressive theological idea. We love God with our minds only.

Yvonne Goulet

Mr. Loomis and others have noted that a truly incarnational worship would use the body as well (and as fully) as the mind. In truly incarnational worship, the celebrant and commentator and lector would not be afraid to smile or even laugh aloud. They would not be afraid to comment casually in greeting the congregation on the things that happened that day that predispose us to worship. The celebrant in an incarnational liturgy would not fear to interject appropriate comments into the worship itself.

An incarnational liturgy would not be content with husbands and wives shaking hands stiffly. A brief embrace would seem appropriate.

Incarnation means that the love of God enters our bodies, our hearts, that we are able to feel that God loves us as well as belive that. One of the ways this sense can be achieved is a greater attention to the body, to the concrete and to the emotions in liturgy.

An incarnational liturgy would involve, sometimes, liturgical dance, in which the body expresses the feelings of reverence and awe that worship inspires.

Incarnational liturgy might, on occasion, ask the people to lift their hands in praise or prayer, or to take hands as they pray.

We need desperately to be freed, liberated, released from the stiff formalism of our worship.

What are the reasons for our formalism? Why, for example, is there so little spontaneity in the Mass? Why do the homilies so seldom have the events in the headlines or in the neighborhood as their subject, or at least as illustrations of the text? Why do homilists resist disclosing something about themselves in their talks? So often, it is the risk of describing a personal event that transforms the Word into flesh for the congregation.

This formalism permeates the whole of liturgy, from celebrant down to the least participant. But there is a need to go beyond this formalism. Members of the congregation should not do the gestures of the Mass because they are told to, but as their way of becoming part of the event. We need to internalize the ritual of the Mass, to incarnate ourselves as Christians at worship. We should participate wholly because this is the way we enflesh the Word.

Why is there such a fear of the body in worship? Why do so many people consider liturgical dance unsuitable, too worldly? Why are women sometimes asked to wear gowns when they appear on the altar as lectors or eucharistic ministers? Is it because an attractive woman (indeed perhaps all women) is seen as a sexual being whereas men are perceived (at least by men) as assexual? And are these complex matters also related to the exclusion of women from Church office?

All of these attitudes and fears suggest the degree to which Puritanism, through Jansenism, has affected the American Church. (I speak of my own experience as an easterner, of course.) The reason,

I believe, is that we have not accepted, or cannot accept the goodness of all of God's creation. We may accept this goodness, (including that of our own bodies) on a theoretical, abstract level, but our instincts and emotions tell us that bodies are not very nice.

No wonder we have lost the ability to celebrate the holiness in every creature, of our own bodies.

Our God, some may think, is a bit of a libertine. Nature, for example, is rife with sex and violence. And Jesus tells us that this God of Nature is also our Father, who knows us more intimately than we know ourselves, that he has numbered even the hairs of our heads. Moreover, this God cares individually about creatures other than humans. He knows each sparrow's fall. He knows each pigeon, each leaf, each blade of grass. He knows each of these creatures in its uniqueness, its individuality.

Original sin, (as well as Jansenism, of course), has warped our view of fleshliness and of the material world. We see creation not in its pristine freshness, but stained by sin.

Of course, we believe that Nature is good and that our bodies are temples of the Spirit, and that even the less than lovely parts are good and beautiful, but we don't seem to experience this goodness.

Control, formality, head consciousness define our worship. We seem to emphasize discipline, order, control, to the detriment of spontaneous outpourings. There is a fear of the body and spontaneity in worship. The training we receive about harnessing our fleshly instincts (and who did not receive such training?) creates this fear of self expression, of self disclosure.

Perhaps the formality of worship was, in part, a reaction against misuses in the early Church of the charismatic gifts. But charismatic renewal is creating people who are not afraid of spontaneity, not afraid of praising God with hands upraised. I wonder if many have not rejected renewal more because of style than because of substance. A healthy use of the charisms can help make worship more incarnational.

A greater attention to the body in worship would point out that incarnation is a serious, practical matter. We would become increasingly aware that there is no separation of liturgy and life, that our loving encounters with one another, in or outside church, are sacramental, grace-giving.

At a recent parish council meeting in my parish, the reading was from the beginning of the Letter of Paul to the Ephesians. The essence of the passages is as follows: "Blessed be God the Father of Our Lord Jesus Christ, who has blessed us with spiritual blessings of heaven in Christ. Before the world was made, he chose us, chose us in Christ to be holy and spotless and live through love in his presence. . . ."

Reflecting on this passage, our pastor spoke of a woman shut-in who refused the offer to receive Communion frequently because it would have been brought to her by a lay person. Accepting the Eucharist from a lay person, the priest pointed out, meant for this woman, that she would have to confront and accept her own holiness as well as that of the other person. Unable to see herself as worthy of holding the Eucharist, she simply refused to receive.

This situation, repeated countless times, is sad. It is possibly related to the refusal of so many women to accept the notion of other women as priests. Unable to see themselves as holy, seeing themselves as shameful, they resist the notion of ordinary men and women as holy. (It is undoubtedly the same reasoning that makes many laypeople resist the notion of a married clergy. Sexual activity is seen as incompatible with holiness, and holiness is seen as necessary for a sacred office.)

How distorted our sense of ourselves is. We must come really to feel good about our bodies, not to fear them and their functions. God made our bodies and he made sex. He intends us to become holy just as we are. He intends us to be Eucharist for one another. He expects Christ to live again in each of us.

We must end this sense of unworthiness, this sense of caste, which separates men and women, laity and clergy, and which has resulted in an unhealthy elevation of the male, celibate, clerical caste.

Only through a healthy acceptance of incarnation, only when laypeople recognize and accept their own holiness, will priests be able to be themselves, share their humanity, their vulnerability with the people. And only then will all people be able to fulfill their priestly role.

Yvonne Goulet

BORN CATHOLIC

"When, then, I ask myself why I am a Catholic, the first reason that occurs to me is that by the grace of God I am one. I am a Catholic because I was born in a Catholic family; because I inherited the faith from a Catholic father and mother, and from their ancestors before them; so far as I know, I have no non-Catholic blood in my veins."

Archbishop Goodier, S.J.
Why I Am and Why I Am Not a Catholic

I'VE often thought that being born Catholic is somewhat like being given a cure for a disease you don't know you have. Before one could pronounce the words, one used to struggle with notions such as sin, guilt, repentance, redemption, reparation, grace. The terms seem to have much more meaning for those who come to them after years of struggle than

they do for those who grew up with them.

Essentially, Catholic Christianity is a religion for adults. It is for people who anguish about their misdeeds, who feel a need for redemption, who long for meaning and community.

Being born Catholic is like standing in an art museum looking at a painting close up. It is only by gaining perspective, by standing a few feet away, that one can make some pattern out of what appears to be blobs of color. With Catholicism, one has to have been able to enflesh the principles with real life experiences, one has to have suffered a bit, to ask profound questions.

Truth is one, but our perception of truth varies as we age. We can better grasp truth as we change. Sometimes, I go back to places where I lived as a small child. The most vivid impression now is how small everything is by comparison with the way I remembered it. The places hadn't diminished, but I had grown. My perspective as a child was of a world I was quite overwhelmed by.

Our perspective changes, but if what we've been exposed to has permanent value, we will be able to grasp it from an adult point of view even though we missed it as a child. This is true of reading serious literature. There are some books and films which we can appreciate as a child on one level, but appreciate all the more profoundly as adults. A work of art has a depth and range of meaning that is inexhaustible and we can be further enriched by each exposure. One can contrast this experience with re-reading at an adult level, as escapist work. Its value will have diminished as one grows, because its value was limited to begin with.

So, becoming a Catholic is not just being born one. If a Catholic Christian does not allow his power of perception to grow, if he or she is not open to looking at old things in new ways, his Christ life cannot grow. Our life is like clay. The Lord wants to mold it. But a certain pliability, a certain flexibility is required.

Many born Catholics, however, seem to feel that adulthood precludes membership in the Church, that belief in Jesus and his Church is something to be put away along with toys and fairy tales.

In a sense, coming to terms with the Church as an adult is similar to coming to terms with one's parents. As one grows, there is a gradual lessening of parental ties, a continual growth and alteration in the relationship until, as an adult, the person feels no real dependency. Often a kind of interdependency occurs, or as parents age, the parents become dependent on the children.

If he or she is unable to let go, and allow the child to grow, the parent may well be faced with rebellion. If the child remains dependent, he will never establish his own identity.

Either way, an unhealthy situation exists.

But an important part of growing up is forgiving one's parents for their own limitations and their failures with us. Most parents try very hard to do what is right. If they make the wrong decisions, we often bear the scars. But it is childish to blame one's parents all one's life for one's own defects. Adulthood means taking responsibility for one's life.

A parent may have behaved a certain way because his parent mistreated him. The cycle can be broken by someone who takes hold and refuses to continue a destructive pattern. For example, a parent who was abused as a child can decide not to mistreat his child.

So, becoming an adult Catholic means establishing a new kind of relationship with the Church. It means not letting one's religion stay at a childish level. It means overcoming a kind of dependency on the Church which obviates adult decision-making.

Often people who are fully adult in their professions and other undertakings, prefer their religion at the childish level. Their religion is static, spiritual. It is a comfort to them rather than a goad. It is a system of answers that prevents them from dealing with existential questions. Religion, for them is closed, a package, rather than open, living, dynamic.

I'm not sure what percentage of Catholics prefer their religion to stay at this childish level. I do know I hear many Catholics, priests and lay people alike, explain away their inability to accept a new approach on the basis of their "training." It was as if Catholicism for some, insulated them against growing.

But Jesus told us that, unless we become as little children we cannot enter the Kingdom of Heaven. Is there, therefore, a difference between being childish and being childlike? Most certainly. It is also said that we must be as wise as serpents and as guileless as doves. In the guilelessness is our childlikeness. In the wisdom is our adulthood.

The childlike dimension, I think, comes in developing a trust in Providence. This is a freeing rather than a binding act. Believing that we are loved and cared for means our life becomes a partnership with the creator, whose grace will fill up our own deficiencies.

The adult dimension is becoming responsible for one's own acts, taking charge of one's growth, seriously attempting to deepen awareness of the meaning of life and one's own gifts and mission.

Our adult dimension should impel us to attempt great things, while our childlike dimension will allow us to remain humble and little. A sense of loving dependence on God is in no way incompatible with taking charge of one's life.

What Catholics need, of course, what all people need, is conversion. Conversion does not mean changing one's religion necessarily (though it may mean that, even for some Catholics). It is a turning toward God. It is not a once-for-all process, but one that is required of us periodically throughout adult life.

As we deal with adult responsibilities, we become hurt. We build walls around ourselves to shield us from further hurt. A sensitive person can perceive the wall in another, sense the hurt that caused it. Persons inside walls can be said to have a certain hardness of heart. Hard-hearted people are, for the most part, very unhappy. The same qualities they need to open up to others are the same ones that allow them to perceive the wonder and beauty of the world. A person behind a wall desperately wants to break out, even though he may not be aware of his imprisonment.

We all build up such walls, at various times in our lives. We become afraid of relationships, of taking risks. Breaking down the wall is conversion. It is transforming our hearts of stone into hearts of flesh so that the word of God can be heard.

I do not believe in giving up on people. I think

people of any age and any circmstances are able to respond to the possibility of redemption, salvation, repentance. There is always the power of grace that is stronger than any other power.

Conversion may take place in any number of ways. It may be a homily that makes one suddenly aware that the Gospel requires something of us. It may be a film or a book. I can remember seeing the film *Quo Vadis*, about the first Christians, when I was fourteen and recognizing for the first time that the first Christians were flesh and blood people as I was.

For many young people, plays such as *Godspell* and *Jesus Christ Superstar* can cause conversion, a new opening up to what they have heard so many times before as children. The experiences can provide a new entrance of faith into feelings as well as thought.

It has been pointed out that the years from 18 to 22 are crucial in many peoples' lives. These are the years when life decisions are made and during which one usually either ratifies or rejects the faith that was taught him as a child. This is a necessary step if childish faith is to become adult faith, and the kind of influences one experiences during these four years may be critical in determining the direction of a person's faith life. That is an important reason for sustaining campus ministers. They are of great importance to Catholic college students.

The adult mode of being Catholic, I think, means putting the Church into its proper perspective. Adult Christians look for truth not in one place, but everywhere. It has been said that truth, whatever its source, is of the Holy Spirit.

Being an adult Catholic, means developing a style of one's own. It means that Jesus didn't promise us a rose garden, that Catholicism is no guarantee of a trouble-free life. It means not accepting Church teaching uncritically. It means not relying on a set of answers to life's problems that was provided in the Baltimore Catechism.

Being an adult Catholic means acquiring an incarnational sense, seeing that faith is worked out in every day life, where we try to perceive what the Gospel means. It is not in expecting miracles, but understanding that God tends to work largely through the natural world. He is unlikely to heal us directly, more likely to heal us through a physician. He is unlikely to speak to us in visions, more likely to speak to us through other human beings. But to listen for the voice of God everywhere and at all times is approaching Christian adulthood.

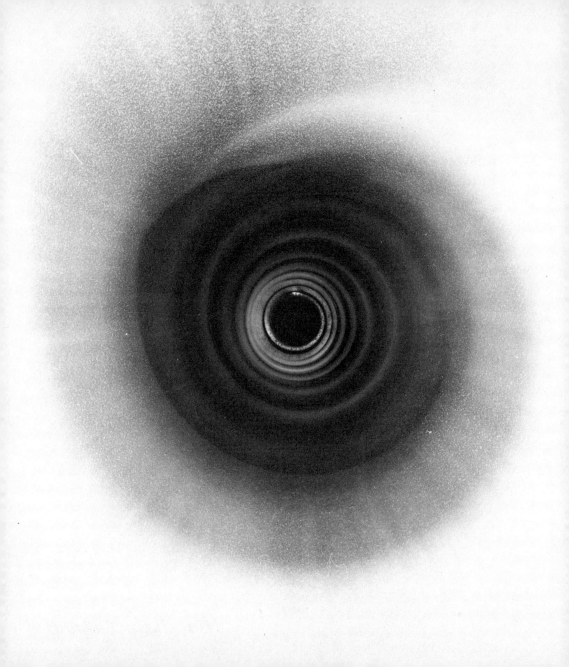

CHOOSING THE CHURCH

"The crucial question is whether a man escapes from the life of his time into a realm of abstraction—it is then that the angst is engendered in human consciousness—or confronts modern life determined to confront its evils and support what is good in it. The first decision then leads to another: is man the helpless victim of transcendental and inexplicable forces, or is he a member of a human community in which he can play a part, however small, toward its modification and reform?"

Lukacs
The Historical Novel

ONE of my favorite contemporary authors is John Fowles, the Englishman. The above quotation from Lukacs is quoted in John Fowles' novel *Daniel Martin.*

Yvonne Goulet

The quotation is central to an understanding of that work, and I think it also is central to the modern predicament: how to find meaning in one's life. In *Daniel Martin*, one of the chief characters, Jane, dallies with the Church as a young woman, marries a stuffy Catholic academic, and remains in this Church while he lives. Widowed, she is attracted to Marxism, but eventually discovers that, for her, no systems work, that she must synthesize her own vision out of the experiences of her life.

The great temptation of membership in the Catholic Church, is, I think, precisely the one Jane experiences. Membership in the Church often means believing in the system, giving assent to a series of abstractions which provide answers to ultimate questions and thereby free the person from the uncomfortable quest.

Many Catholics, I think, let the system or the abstractions rule their lives. They never go beyond the basic questions and answers into any existential struggle with belief and experience, synthesizing a belief for his or her particular life.

To accept the system rather than confront life's multiplicity, is, I think, a failure of incarnation. Again, in the television program from *The Long Search* on the Catholic Church, English Catholic Judith Dryhurst, a convert, discusses the tension that must prevail in a healthy belief: "There are times when you want the answers given to you. . . . But that's a very immature conception of religion. There's enormous ferment in the Church and people . . . who constantly question the statements by the Vatican. That doesn't mean we reject the authority of the Church. It's just that, in a growing and developing Church . . . you look at it and question it." She later states, "In a search for equilibrium, balance, it's marvelous to have a structure there."

That, I think, is a very healthy adult mode of being a member of the Catholic Church. The notion of balance is important to me too, and the wonder of membership in the Church is that one has the two poles—the teachings of the Church, and one's own experiences. We need both to reach some kind of understanding of the Gospel in our lives. Without careful attention to an evaluation of our own experiences, we become slavish followers of a system, lose incarnation. Without the teachings of the Church, there is a danger in making the Gospel in one's own image.

I see my own membership in the Church as a kind of love/hate relationship. While I have never had any serious doubts about the Lordship of Jesus, I am frequently very angry with the institutional Church, and have been sorely tempted to leave it.

I stay because I continue to ratify my membership. I realize that belonging is an entirely voluntary matter, and that no sanctions would be invoked should I decide to leave.

But I stay and hope I will receive the grace always to stay. Belonging to the institutional Church, is, for me, part of incarnation. Again the insights of Judith Dryhurst are appropriate: "I'm quite sure what I was searching for, before I became a Catholic, was the security of belonging to what I believe is the closest thing to what Jesus wanted the Church to be."

I feel that way. Although I did not choose the Church in quite the same way a convert does, after a long search, I nevertheless have rethought my faith, and continue to rethink it in terms of new information, new scholarship, new insights and experiences. Jesus, I think, meant us to be part of a believing community, however imperfect. It is in my commitment to community that I am committed to him. Withholding myself from a community would be a judgment, an act of pride, the implication that I can pursue holiness and fulfill the Gospel apart from a community of faith.

I can be irritated with my local Church, my parish, but I cannot reject it, or give up on it. The territorial parish, I think, is a great invention. It is rooted in the land, in the earth, there is a certain geographical imperative. The geographical parish, I think, is the guarantor (for the most part) of universality in the parish. There is more of a possibility that I will encounter all kinds of people there than if I go to a parish of my choosing. It is precisely in attempting to create community out of diversity that incarnation occurs. If I go merely where the liturgies are more suitable, the educational level higher, the political bent more in keeping with mine, I am rejecting those things in my geographical church, when incarnation means coming to terms with them.

The territorial parish is a reflection of what Southern writers call "a sense of place." The rootedness that was once found in neighborhoods must now be found in parishes. That is why parishes must become a center in people's lives of cultural and recreational undertakings as well as spiritual ones.

To Live God's Word

It is in the parish that, most probably, one experiences community. One learns to draw strength there and to give strength.

But rootedness in a particular parish is not enough. I personally need to belong to a world-wide structure. No other structure is as truly world-wide, and, therefore, as truly communal as the Church. I find the body of Christ in all its manifestations in the universal Church.

Despite my general assent, my feelings about the Church vary.

At times, I experience great pride and joy. During the deaths and elections of Popes in 1978, I was proud to belong to the oldest institution in the world.

I think the Church, as a force for peace and justice, with its worldwide structure, is the key means of building the Kingdom. It is the only organization, one newsman said, which has branch offices all over the earth. Of course this potential is largely unrealized even within the Church. There is great disparity between the Church's preachings about justice and its actions. But it preaches a pure truth, and all of us are responsible for seeing it made flesh.

Having struggled in my own parish with inventing means of structuring committees, I see the Church's very organization a miracle, adequate proof of its divine origin.

The doctrines and dogmas, the Sacraments, the mystical tradition, the teachings about, and action in behalf of, charity and justice, are all sources of pride. And the Church's resiliency, as manifested in Vatican II, is a sign of its ability to rejuvenate, to respond to the times.

On reflection, one comes to see that the Church's visibility, its material dimension, is perhaps the truest demonstration of incarnation. I could never be content belonging to an invisible church.

The Church's sacramental system, however poorly administered and inadequately understood, nevertheless touches people at all the junctures of their lives, an absolutely essential ministry to the flesh and blood people of God.

And authority, no matter how much I rail against specific teachings and decisions, is important to me. I was and am attracted to the Protestant Episcopal Church. But in 1975, I covered for our diocesan paper, *Church World*, the convention of the Episcopal Bishops in Portland, Maine. The liturgies were exquisite and I was pleased with the Bishops' openness on such matters as women's ordination, but when it came to moral teaching, there was no unanimity. The Bishops simply did not know what to say about abortion, for example. There was no final authority. And that Church seems not to know what to say as a body on many matters.

In that experience, I discovered how central authority is for me. I may not agree, but there must be a firm voice. Listening to that voice will help me form my own opinion. But I cannot be thrown simply

on my own resources. The tension between authority and conscience, I find, is absent outside the
Catholic Church.

There are, of course, some things wrong with the
way I learned my faith. Having spent 14 years in
Catholic schools (in the forties, fifties, and sixties) I
learned a largely vertical religion. I was more
aware of my obligation to worship Jesus than to
follow him. I was and am more bothered by small
sins of commission rather than big sins of omission. I
am struggling to learn the real place of guilt, to deal
with guilt constructively, and to look at myself primarily as a saint rather than a sinner.

But the Church didn't do such a bad job with me.
With all the bad baggage, it gave me Jesus, and in
learning more about him under the tutelage of an
awakened Church, I am getting out from under all
the legalisms and becoming the free child of God I
was meant to be.

I still find the Church too legalistic and think we

need to go a long way in discerning how the spirit of the law should guide us as an institution.

The individual Catholic Christian, I think, must struggle with the place of the Church in his life. The Church is often too much with us. If Flannery O'Connor's Southerner is "Christ-haunted," the American Catholic tends to be "Church-haunted," and many adult Catholics, on becoming adult, reject the Church as irrelevant to their adult status.

The Church, no matter how important, is only one element in my life, even in my Christ life—a life in which I make the decisions, choose the direction, construct a moral vision and try to be faithful to myself. I am convinced Jesus meant it that way. He is in me as much as in the Church. And the Christian life is not about obeying the Church, but about trying to live Christ in my own circumstances.

Fr. Bryan Hehir of the United States Catholic Conference, in his talks on the Church's teachings on justice, speaks of the "scandal of particularity" in

Yvonne Goulet

Jesus, that the almighty God chose to be born with human limitations. Our scandal too is particularity, that tension between our infinite longing for peace and love and truth and justice, and our own sinfulness, laziness, stupidity.

The human condition, that of animals with infinite longings, is surely God's biggest joke. But he loves his funny valentine, and he smiles at us. He loves us enough to have become one of us, one with us, so we must never forget to laugh at the incongruities in our lives as well as pray about them.

There is a saying that the only things we can give our children are roots and wings. The Church of my youth gave me roots, but I am having to learn to fly on my own. No matter how fast, or how far I fly, however, I always seem to return to my roots.

Part II

COMMUNICATING

Yvonne Goulet

WORDS

"Do we not know that we are inarticulate? That is what defeats us. It is our inability to communicate to one another how we are locked within ourselves, unable to say the simplest thing of importance to one another, any of us, that makes our lives like those of a litter of kittens in the woodpile, that gives the physician, and I don't mean the highpriced psychoanalyst, his opportunity; psychoanalysis amounts to another dialectic into which to be locked.

"The physician enjoys a wonderful opportunity to witness the words being born. Their actual colors and shapes are laid before him, carrying their tiny burdens which he is privileged to take into his care with their unspoiled newness. He may see the difficulty with which they have been born and what they are destined to do. No

one else is present but the speaker and our-
selves and we have been the words' very
parents. Nothing is more moving.''

William Carlos Williams
The Autobiography of William Carlos Williams

MUCH of life is about communication. It seems
ironic therefore, that we go through life with such
meager vocabularies, such "shabby equipment"
(Eliot's term) with which to convey our thoughts and
feelings to the world.

If incarnation means the word becoming flesh, it
also means that the flesh must be made word, that
we must learn to communicate our thoughts and
feelings accurately, and that we must be perceptive
of and receptive to the thoughts and feelings of
others.

In his autobiography, poet William Carlos Williams speaks of his unique position as both physician

and man of letters. His work as a physician, he explained, was largely involved with listening, with helping patients find the words, to go beyond the obvious to what was really bothering them.

Throughout the work, Williams criticizes what he calls dialectics: ". . . the hunted news I get from patients' eyes is not trivial. It is profound: whole academics of learning, whole ecclesiastical hierarchies are founded upon it and have developed what they call their dialectic upon nothing else, their lying dialectics. A dialectic is any arbitrary system which, since all systems are mere inventions, is necessarily in each case a false premise, upon which a closed system is built, shutting those who combine themselves to it from the rest of the world."

Williams, in all his work, is fiercely opposed to institutions, systems. This opposition is most graphically demonstrated in his long poem, "Paterson," in which the burning of the library symbolizes the destruction of systems.

Contrasted with the systems approach, which categorizes and pigeonholes people, treating them all as cases, as in the social sciences, is the kind of attention to each person which allows Williams to perceive his or her uniqueness, "catching the evasive life of the thing," perceiving what is really being said by each one.

What Williams discerns, from all his careful looking and listening, is the expression of the self, what is attempting to be said, the awareness of how we all struggle with words, attempting to articulate our deepest needs and meanings: "For under the language which we have been listening to all our lives a new, a more profound language underlying all the dialectics offers itself. It is what we call poetry. That is the final phase."

In view of our focus on incarnation, there are

three points to be reflected on in Williams' concepts. The first is about systems and institutions themselves. (See the chapters on Institutions I and II). More pertinent to the present reflection is his discussion of listening which penetrates the inarticulate barriers which surround people, and the concept of the insufficiency of language as it is usually used.

But incarnation is the flesh attempting to become word. Without the words, we are imprisoned in our own flesh. With the power of the word not only can we reflect better on our own experiences, but we can break out of our prisons, share our experiences and observations with others.

As Williams says, the final phase is poetry, people finding the words they need to express themselves. Incarnation is helping the words to be born. This demands not only a love of words, but attention to the person and the moment.

Truly incarnational encounters with others transcend what is commonly called "sharing." They are listening and speaking at a deeper level. They cannot be labeled and categorized. Incarnation attends to the irreplaceability of this person, this time.

All of us are physicians, privileged, like Williams, in our best moments, to watch the words being born. We can all give birth to possibilities in one another. We go beyond structures, systems, dialectics which are the formal, ordered, scientific ways of dealing with life's problems. We go with the moment. We allow our attention to be focused. We listen to what another person may not even know he or she is trying to say. We help the words be born with our attention, our respect, our belief in their possibility.

This kind of I-Thou encounter will not happen every time we go to the supermarket, but it may happen at the most unexpected times. It means we must let our own barriers down, convey to others that we are approachable. Once in a while, we are in a situation where the poetry can come to the surface.

But language itself is a barrier. And an English teacher perhaps more than a doctor has the opportunity to help the words being born. A teacher can, by trying to find the right words, by trying for precision and poetry in the choices of words, help others reflect on what they think, and what they feel, how they experience things.

Jargon must be avoided at all costs. Religious educators and all educators get into systems, think about numbers, using the jargon rather than trying to express freshly exactly what is happening. Using cliches and jargon is deadly. Only expressing ourselves freshly can we ever discover the nuances of our thought and perceptions. We are all poets at heart, or at least all have a touch of the poet, a wellspring of the imagination to provide fresh words.

Williams, in the same work mentioned above, makes another point about how difficult it is to

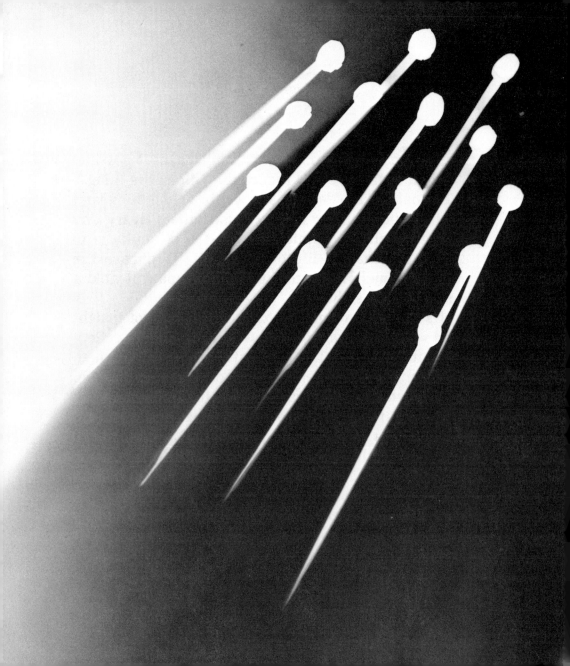

grasp the moment and how writing makes it possible for him to capture and record the "life of the thing." He speaks of the demands of writing, "the thing isn't to find the time for it—we waste hours every day doing absolutely nothing at all—the difficulty is to catch the evasive life of the thing, to phrase the words in such a way that the stereotype will yield a moment of insight."

I suspect that most of us have flashes of insight and wisdom frequently if we leave time for reflection in our lives. The moment of insight is hard to pinpoint. Such moments tend to come at inopportune times, when one is teaching, or in the middle of a hockey game, when one is brushing one's teeth or soaking in a bathtub. The point is to pin the moment down, enflesh it, hold on to it, to say it. A word is not dead when it is said. It only begins to live then.

Much of incarnation consists in grasping these moments of insight and trying to remember them. Wordsworth called the basis of poetry emotion "recollected in tranquillity." We may have the emotion, which is a quite specific event related to a finite specific cause. Reflecting on it is the basis of the poem, whether the poem will be printed on a page or remain only in the heart and mind. Incarnation then means not only recognizing such moments in our own minds and preserving them, but also helping others to learn the technique in their own lives.

As a teacher, I find that in helping others to find the poem in their own lives, it is important that they come to love words, that they reverence words, not only as functional, conveying meaning, but for their form, their sound. A word can be appreciated in many ways and it is only when they come together with the insight and the order, that poetry, as we know it results.

Writing, of its very essence, is an attempt at incarnation. The word, we hope, is made flesh when it is read and listened to and responded to by someone. We try, but one's equipment is always disordered. As T.S. Eliot says in "East Coker," from *Four Quartets:*

> "and so each venture
> Is a new beginning, a raid on the inarticulate
> With shabby equipment always deteriorating
> In the general mess of imprecision of feeling,
> Undisciplined squads of emotion."

How difficult it is to "catch the evasive life of the thing," to record and reflect on it. But memory, it is said, is the faculty which forgets, and our insights, unless they are recorded, are fleeting.

Our own experiences, our own insights, are the very material that can help others find the truths about their own lives. The reasons homilies are often so deadly is that few clergymen either take the time to reflect on their insights, or if they do record the insights, dare to share them with others. Homilies, teaching, any kind of official or unofficial interacting with others, requires insight and self-disclosure. If we are not willing to disclose ourselves, to share our humanity with others, it is unlikely they will share theirs with us.

Incarnation means entering into the lives of other people. We cannot stand outside the world's problems as they occur in individual men and women and still hope to bring the word to them. Yeast, it has been said, must be within bread and not along side it.

Eucharist is a sign and effect of the total communication of ourselves to others. It is what is demanded of us, to be broken for others. This is not to say we must be irrational, or sentimental, or masochistic. We must be discreet, knowing when the situation calls for such communication. It is essentially availability, openness to others.

Yvonne Goulet

Words are all we have for communicating with one another. Our life is a continual struggle to find the right words, to express ourselves exactly, and to hear what is being said beneath the words. It is a lifelong effort.

THE ARTS

". . . the same forces that have destroyed the mystery of holiness have destroyed the mystery of beauty."

Herbert Read
"The Necessity of Art"
The Arts and Man

THE Catholic Church needs beauty. The liturgies of the past may have been obscure, the statues sentimental, but there nevertheless was in the pageantry of vestments, incense, monstrances, Gregorian chant, a festival of the senses that many children would not have been exposed to anywhere else in their experience.

Occasionally, now, one comes to such beauty in the Church. Occasionally, one sees a modern church building that is beautiful, whole lines and colors and design uplift the spirit. I can think of one or two such modern buildings. One is the huge church on the grounds of St. Anselm's College in Manchester, New Hampshire. Another is the chapel on the grounds of the Franciscan monastery in Kennebunkport, Maine.

Occasionally, one hears modern works sung by a competent choir. Once in a while one hears the liturgy incarnated by the celebrant, so that the words are made his own. Now and then one hears a lector who reads the word of God so that it is heard. But seldom, so seldom do these things happen. So seldom are we specialists at the one thing we must do, worship.

The liturgy must be nourished by the principles of excellence and the techniques of visual and dramatic art.

Art essentially orders reality. Because of the artist's vision, reality is seen in a new perspective. This is manifested well in Wallace Stevens' poem:

To Live God's Word

I placed a jar in Tennessee
And round it was, upon a hill.
It made that slovenly wilderness
Surround that hill.

It is the function of art, the man-made object, to organize the slovenliness of nature. By focusing our vision on the reality of nature in a new way, we can learn to appreciate nature in a new way, noticing its form, color, design. A Wyeth painting, for example, far from taking us away from nature, should give us a new appreciation of its wonders, should show us how to look at a thing.

The very essence of art is this order, this selectivity, this ability to express a number of things by a shadow, a line, a word, a phrase of music.

The impulse to holiness is exactly the same as the impulse to beauty. Great poetry, it has been said, makes us want to pray. Great painting and sculpture and music should make us want to celebrate, to worship.

The reason holiness brings us to beauty and beauty to holiness is that they are two faces of truth. Truth is found in religion and art, and religion and art need each other. They keep each other orthodox, centered in the possibilities of the human. Without religion, art becomes solipistic. Without art, religion becomes a dry exercise. The human person, consisting of body and soul, needs to have his soul touched through his body. Christian faith, let it be said again, though grounded in the divine made human, situated in a visible Church, and made concrete in sacraments, has the constant temptation of focusing only on the unseen and of becoming one with its own legalisms.

What can be more concrete than art, consisting of color, form, word, texture. It appeals simultaneously to the senses, imagination, intellect, and spirit. It

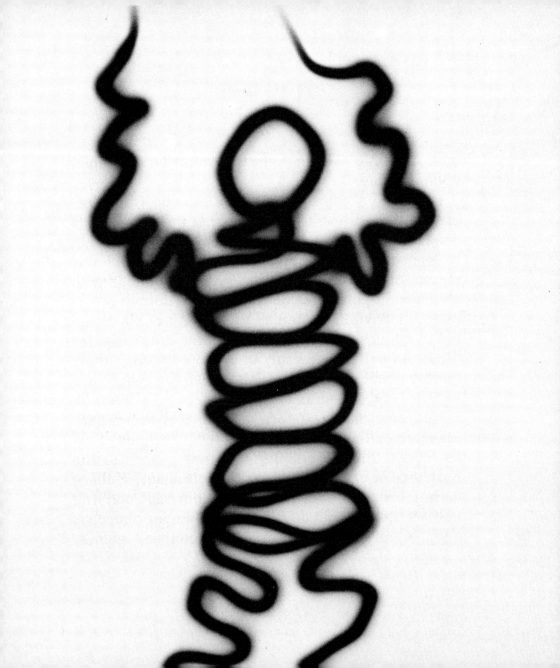

communicates what otherwise would be ineffable, inexpressible.

One of the reasons I believe we, as Catholics, often fail to enflesh the word, is that there is so little good religious art, and that we have not been taught to appreciate good art. Bad art reinforces our stereotypes the same way homilies filled with cliches and platitudes do. Bad art reinforces prejudices. It trivializes, tames the reality of Christian life in all its splendor. And most of what passes for Christian art is incredibly bad. How can one think freshly about the truths of faith when the images are so trite, corny, sentimental?

And how many pastors or liturgical committees take it upon themselves to teach the principles of art as reflected in the building of a new church or the purchase or crafting of a new appointment? If there were more awareness of what comprises good and bad art there would be more beauty in our churches and less of the "emporer's new clothes" games, where everyone pretends the new church and its appointments are beautiful because they cost so much.

There should be a strong, concerted effort by liturgical committees everywhere to insist on art objects consistent with the faith they are intended to reflect—strong, beautiful, valuable, enduring, made with love and skill. There should be nothing mass-produced, plastic, temporary about worship. A certain seriousness about what we do and how we do it is necessary.

Another step in incarnation would be to have religious education give close attention to the Church's art heritage. Exposure to the truly beautiful would perhaps be the best insurance against the ugliness and insipidness of what passes for much of Christian Catholic art and architecture.

What principles might be used in teaching art to Catholics? The central theme of incarnation should be grasped, and the point made that the materials with which we surround ourselves must result from both vision and craftsmanship. A work of art should be evaluated not only in terms of its statement, but in terms of the skill and love with which it is crafted.

And we should stop pretending when the emperor is wearing nothing. No longer should the sacraments be seen to function *ex opere operato.* No longer should their human dimension be ignored. As a matter of fact, the sacraments should be worked into the events of our lives in concrete ways, using the materials of our lives. All of the physical, material events of Church life should be seen as times to teach about God infusing his spirit into time and place.

In sculpture and painting. Christians must be made to realize that representational images are not absolutely necessary, that a degree of abstraction can help us focus on the reality being communicated. And the horrors of sentimentality should be described (if possible) without offending those who cling to this kind of representation.

Similarly with liturgical music. While there is room for folk as well as serious music, and for traditional as well as modern, standards should be observed, in terms of performance as well as composition. Anything does not go in liturgy, and to use material that is inherently bad because for example, "it appeals to youth," I think is pandering to, rather than serving, the people.

Ideally the arts should express in a sensuous way the intimations of immortality that are otherwise inexpressible. And if the audience for good art in the Church is not present, then building the audience for art should be a priority.

Yvonne Goulet

THE CREATIVE DREAMER

"The world is full of frustrated artists, or rather of people whose creative instincts have been frustrated."

Herbert Read
"The Necessity of Art"
The Arts and Man

THE works of Tennessee Williams abound with characters critics refer to as "creative dreamers." Maggie, for example, in the play *Cat on a Hot Tin Roof* solves several problems by the little white lie that she is pregnant. She gives her husband, whose masculinity has been suspect, a new confidence in himself, and she gives his dying father "Big Daddy" hope of grandchildren and, therefore, of immortality.

The ability to dream creatively, to invent possible outcomes of situations, to envision things that do not currently exist, is possibly the most underrated and underdeveloped quality in the human person. It is not that only a few people have creative powers. We are all born with them; they are part of the human equipment. Everyone, according to the playwright Eugene O'Neill has a "touch of the poet," the possibility of living creatively.

It is a real challenge then, to discover what is the basis of the atrophy of the imagination, why there is so little originality and creativity, and how it can be rediscovered to make our society more human.

It is Herbert Read's contention, in the article mentioned above, that the decline in creativity is the result of the decline in attention to sensation. "If seeing and handling, touching and hearing, and all the refinements of sensation that developed historically in the conquest of nature and the manipulation of material substances are not educed and trained from birth to maturity, the result is a being that hardly deserves to be called human: a dull-eyed, bored and listless automaton whose one desire is for violence in some form or other—violent action, violent sounds, distractions of any kind that can penetrate to its deadened nerves.

Anyone who has ever faced a classroom of teen-agers on Monday morning with the task of helping them to: 1) understand and 2) enjoy literature, can identify with the notion of "dull-eyed, bored and listless automatons" who resist the plunge into liter-ature. Often the most common adjective of the tele-vision generation is "boring." Anything that re-quires attention for more than a brief period is incomprehensible to some.

Some of the most accomplished seem to lack a spark and those with vitality seldom channel it into their studies. There are lively young people who care little for ideas, studious ones who have little vitality. Who has failed them and how? Why has that energy not been challenged and channeled by studies?

To Live God's Word

I think Read's diagnosis is accurate. The young have lost the power of sensation which is everyone's birthright. Because the touching, looking, listening, smelling abilities have not been developed, they have been lost. And because it is human to want sensation, the young demand the most extreme forms. Sex and drugs and violence are a kind of "high" for those for whom a symphony, or a poem, or a flower are too subtle.

The source of this general deadening, Read maintains, is the industrial society in which we live, in which human activity has become subservient to the machine and the arts and crafts have declined. Add to this situation television and its encouragement of passivity, and you have 17-year-olds who have lost the ability to sense.

The educational system seldom centers around the use of the arts. It is, rather, the handmaid to information processing. The pace of society makes the requisite contemplative stance toward nature impossible. Even the notion of a "natural high" is foreign to many people.

The loss of sensation and, thus, of creativity, is not the fault of the young, but their misfortune. However, with a determined effort, led perhaps by educators and the Church, it may be possible to reinstate opportunities to 1) develop the power of sensation and the imagination and 2) provide natural outlets for such impulses.

What does all of this have to do with incarnation? Simply everything. Goodness, as well as beauty, depends on the ability of the human being to see beyond the obvious, to develop insight, to identify with other human beings, to hear what is not being said, to enjoy little things.

Read makes a direct connection between the decline in the arts and the decline of worship. "The decline of religious worship is doubtless the inevitable consequence of a growth of scientific rationalism, and the fact that scientific progress has not

been accompanied by any equivalent progress in ethical standards is frequently regretted. But it is not so often observed that the same forces that have destroyed the mastery of holiness have destroyed the mystery of beauty.''

In my mind, the implication is that a revival of the arts could lead to holiness, and a revival of religion could stimulate the arts.

The glory of God is the human person fully alive. That vitality is measurable by the degree to which a person can take delight in the world, and the degree to which he can create beauty. The creativity does not have to be exercised in the production of art works, although the possibility of creating crafts should be present in every person. A person may simply live in a very creative way, being original in speech, in action. A creative person is an individual, not dependent upon others to set a pattern for living, but free enough, and spontaneous enough to live creatively.

To Live God's Word

Although art is perhaps essentially "aristocrat-ic," (that is, the power to create great works of art is not given to everyone but to the rare few,) never-theless, the possibility of creative thinking and living is within the realm of everyone. Everyone has a unique genetic make up, an irreplaceable set of talents, gifts with which to mirror the divine. God can become incarnate in each person in a perfect, fresh, irreplaceable way, according to the gifts of the individual person. Everyone (except the severely disabled, perhaps) has the power to wonder, to sense, to feel, to respond. The precious few retain that childlike ability to respond with wonder to creation throughout their lives.

It is a great sin that we let this wonder become lost, that we allow children to deaden their ability to respond by endless hours of television watching, by allowing them to use coloring books, and paint-by-number sets.

I think it is a primary task of educators and

Church people to maintain this ability to respond in themselves and in the young. It may be so that the degree to which incarnation is possible in a human being is the degree to which his imaginative powers have remained alive.

Goodness is directly related to this imaginative power. It is only through the exercise of imagination that we can project ourselves into the circumstances of others, can "feel with," can understand what life is like from another person's point of view. Short of direct experience of things, imagination is the way we live vicariously, live many lives. We are all limited in our experiences, but unlimited in our imaginative possibilities. That is why the arts are such a treasure. Through them we can travel, live many lives, experience beauty which otherwise might be cut off from us.

Apart from its benefits to the individual person, imagination is a great resource for society as well. No creative act in the sciences, or in life as well as in the arts was ever done without the exercise of a healthy imagination. It is the source of inventions, of new solutions to the world's problems, of new structures, of new approaches. It is that faculty which allows the appropriate answer to come forth rather than a standard one.

Without imagination, there would only be sameness. People who live in a rut do so often because they never dream of other possibilities. Dreams are the parents of deeds.

The sum total of the sharpening of powers of sensation, attention to the natural world, and the encouragement of the life of the imagination is the creative person.

This creative person, or "creative dreamer," may come in two varieties, the artist and the saint. (Sometimes, as in a person like Thomas Merton, there is a combination.) Both are excellent examples of incarnation. The artist transforms his inspiration into works which endure, and continue, and communicate his vision: a play, a poem, a painting, a musical composition. Such a work exists in time, has a kind of immortality which recreates for each new viewer or hearer the vision of the artist. The artist renders the image. "The essence of any work of art," Read says, is in "realization and manifestation." Read also quotes Cezanne to the effect that the artist "gives concrete shape to sensations and perceptions," that he incarnates them.

If great artists provide images which are the basis of a whole era, the great saints do the same thing. The saint is one who, rather than creating an object, makes concrete his perceptions and sensations about the Gospel in him or herself. The saint lives his vision. His life is his life's work. His genius is sanctity, recognizing the possibilities of goodness and holiness and acting upon them.

But great artists and great saints are models for us, not simply to be admired, but to be imitated. Creativity is within the power of every person. It is part of everyone's humanity. One's ability to create is closely allied with his/her uniqueness, the freedom of his spirit.

Originality is absolutely necessary in every area of life. Each person we encounter is special, unique, a fresh revelation of God. Dealing with each person demands a response to that uniqueness. The physician must call upon his imaginative resources in diagnosing and treating the patient. The teacher, in trying to release each student from the prison of his or her own past, his or her own wounds, must use imagination to set up situations, events, encounters, which will allow the student to open himself up, to show his or her vulnerability, to learn, to change. And how much more true is it for ministers of the Gospel! Sharpened powers of sensitivity, free reign of the imagination are essential in conveying the most sublime truths of all.

How to educate others to this form of incarnation? Herbert Read's answer is education through the arts. I think the arts should be the core of every curriculum, whether secular or religious. Only the arts sustain the human in us, and release the spiritual.

So closely allied are religion and the arts that it is said that reading poetry makes people want to pray. Similarly, a recognition of the truth of the Gospel should make people want to dance, or paint, or write.

Catholic education has traditionally been strong on discipline and scholarship. I think there needs to be an equally strong emphasis on the arts—an emphasis which is totally accurate in view of the centrality of incarnation. The emphasis on the arts in Catholic schools could be the specific difference, (in addition to that of religion) of Catholic schools which helps students grow into liberated, creative adults.

With all our problems, society is desperately in need of creativity. The arts are indisputably the means.

Part III

ACTING

Yvonne Goulet

WHERE IS THE TRUE CHRIST?

> *"Where is the true Christ? On the side of those who are all too ready to situate him in a glorious heaven, in transcendence, in the vertical . . . or on the side of those who find him in the struggle for justice, in man's devotion to man, in the determination to put an end to all forms of alienation?"*
>
> Fr. Herve Chaigne, OFM

WHERE is the true Christ. Of all that he said and did, and of all that is said and done about him, where should the emphasis lie? In doing what do we finally approach the fulfillment of his teachings? Indeed where is the true Christ? And how do we find him? We seem to wait for something in our lives to point the way.

But what are we waiting for? Our lives seem a constant preparation for acting as Christians. When everything is right, we will be ready to serve. When we meet the right person, get the right degree, find the right parish, get the right spiritual director, find the right job, we will be ready for life. But life, as someone said, is what happens to us while we are planning something else.

We wait and prepare for the ideal while life goes by. We wonder about the transcendent God and what he could want of us—when he is speaking through the concrete circumstances of our lives? We think of spiritual perfection while God suffers all around us in the humanity waiting to be healed.

What is true for us individually is true of the Church as well. The Church waits, substituting piety for charity, lost in its formality, unable to see or respond to the suffering Person in its midst. And yet, for many Catholics, it is this very sense of formality, of escape, of enclosure that attracts them.

One pastor of an upper middle class parish explained his parishioners' resistance to attempts at creating a more spontaneous and socially-conscious liturgy. "They don't like it. They're very conservative where change is concerned. They've worked very hard to get where they are, with nice homes and big cars and they want the Church to be the quiet place in their lives. They don't want the Church to remind them that they have obligations beyond attending Mass on Sunday."

He said this in a resigned rather than a judgmental way. But the situation is quite widespread. It's been years since I've heard a homily (virtually the only place the priest can reach people) on social justice. The Church, at the parish level, in my experience, is far more involved with comforting the comfortable than afflicting them, or with comforting the afflicted.

When it was reported a year or so ago that, after Jews, Irish Americans are the most economically successful people in our society (followed by Italian Americans,) I had mixed feelings. Most of these

people undoubtedly had Catholic roots. Has our awareness of the Gospel matched the depth to which we have learned the ways of capitalism? Have we grown in social consciousness as we grow in social standing? Do we have any compunctions about the acquisition of wealth? And do we, in our economic good fortune, want and work for the same rights for the poor and powerless that our grandparents had to struggle for? Is our faith manifested in our passion for justice and equity, or do we close our eyes to the needs of others? Or salve our guilt by a check to United Way or CARE?

The Church, at the parish, diocesan, or universal level should not be a haven. It should be a challenge. We should feel slighly ill at ease, not so much over our sins of commission, but for our sins of omission. What have I not done that I should have done should be a major question.

We have had enough guilt, I think, about sins of sexual morality. Let us concentrate on sins that cause, directly or indirectly, innocent people to suffer.

There is such a terrible fear of taking the plunge (the water would be so cold!) that even the official Church worries about "a reversal of the ontological order which puts humanitarian concerns above the hierarchy of beings and values." It was Pope Paul, in an address on July 10, 1968, who made this emphasis.

The emphasis, I think, is wrong. Of course, Catholic social thought and action must not lose sight of its origin in the Gospel. But if action on behalf of justice is a constitutive dimension of the preaching of the Gospel, as the 1971 Synod of Bishops has said, why is this decision made? Why must social concerns be separated from theological ones? Why is preaching the word seen as separate in any sense, from doing it? Social action for Christians must not be separated from its origins, but neither must the Gospel be separated from social concerns.

Yvonne Goulet

Let us not forget that the central fact of our life is incarnation. What greater reversal of ontological order could there be than that God became man? What more bald example do we have of paradox? Our God is always a God of surprises. "My ways are not your ways."

Following the Gospel means self-emptying, inconvenience, discomfort. Rather than a God of escape, our God is a God of confrontation. He doesn't so much remove suffering from the human race as suffer through us. We become Christian precisely to the extent to which we take the cross on our shoulders. We can't just walk side by side with Christ. We have to walk in him, and he in us.

This incarnational plunge into reality can perhaps be seen in concentric circles. The outside circle might be the Church as we traditionally perceive it, making declarations, dispensing sacraments. The second dimension would be that of those who grasp the Gospel's message of love and try to act with love and concern, who work at the practical ways of the Kingdom. In the inner circle, to complete this Dantean illustration, would be found those who suffer, who share in the sufferings of Christ.

It was Simone Weil, who suffered much in her life, who said, "Suffering: superiority of man over God. We needed the incarnation to keep that from becoming a scandal."

A while ago, in his syndicated column, Fr. Richard McBrien posed a question that points up the disparity between our preaching and our doing. The question he posed is this: If you were a member of a parish council and had just learned from the pastor that there was a $15,000 surplus in this year's budget, how would you vote on its dispersal?" Father McBrien went through the traditional catalogue of cliches, about meeting the needs of the poor, deepening the spirituality of the community or evangelizing the unchurched or reach out to youth. But, he asked, "What do we do about them in the concrete?

Yvonne Goulet

When dollars and cents are involved?''

I think that no matter what the needs of the parish are, I would vote to give the money to the poor, whether directly, or indirectly though some helping agency.

Increasingly, I think groups of Christians, like individual Christians, develop a personality, that certain values prevail. But I think Jesus intended our goods to be used for those most in need.

Giving money away to the poor or the powerless or the handicapped (in essence, to those who suffer) is a great act of love and selflessness for a parish, one that I believe would bring it many blessings. Giving the money away, out of our surplus, is hardly more risky than the act of the widow who gave away all she had, and Jesus blessed rather than criticized her for her economic mismanagement.

Giving the money away to those who suffer is a concrete sign of our commitment to the heart of the

Gospel, loving our fellow men and women. It would be the most beautiful liturgical act, better than any banners that might be bought. It would be the best kind of example to youth, better than many classes in religious education. It would do more to teach the Gospel than any number of new books in the parish library or any number of workshops, or recreational activities. It would do far more for the community than a repaired roof or a new snowblower.

Giving the money away means that we understand the paradox of the Gospel, that we are to give and only thereby receive; it would demonstrate that we acknowledge our responsibility to the poor and powerless of our community, in whom we see the suffering Christ. It means that we are willing and able to lay up a treasure in heaven rather than on earth.

We must begin to incarnate our glowing principles, to give exactly when it hurts, exactly when it is a sacrifice to do so. How much better can a parish teach by what it does, than by what it says, even to its own people.

The fact is that unmerited suffering is redemptive. Those who suffer in our communities are the suffering Christ. They are co-redeemers of the world and all of us will be among the suffering at some time.

It is the glory of those in the second circle that they choose voluntarily to share in the suffering of others. With all our choices, these people and these parishes choose the way of selflessness and love.

If we are not in the inner circle, where the real work is being done, at least we can be in the second circle of those whose sublime vocation it is to be able to help, to minister, like Veronica, to the suffering Christ.

THE POOR

"The coat that hangs in the closet belongs to the poor."

Dorothy Day

HOW should an American Christian live in the latter half of the twentieth century? Does it matter if we consume more food and fuel than our fair share? What should be our goals as Christians? How much should our Christian commitment permeate our life? How can we Christianize our surroundings? What should we eat? Where should we live?

These may seem like irrelevant questions to many Christians. If we give of our goods, what matter is it that we have comfortable lives. Jesus noted that both he (who came eating and drinking) and John the Baptist (who came fasting) were both criticized. Jesus also seemed to discard dietary rules, noting that it is not what goes into a man's mouth, (food) but what comes out of it (slander, etc.) that is sinful.

Jesus is the model of balance. He keeps bringing our attention back to the one thing necessary, the love and service of God and man. Other rules are means to this end and must not become ends in themselves.

So, it seems that there can be no final answers about fasting and feasting. No one can make rules or judgments for another about how much material goods he should acquire and how he should dispose of his belongings.

I get a bit disturbed with self-proclaimed prophets no matter how well motivated. A while ago I sat down to lunch with a follower of Dorothy Day and the Catholic Worker movement. (We happen to be members of the same Government committee). The woman, although well educated and brilliant, is voluntarily poor. She acted that day in her pro-phetic role. Her eyes piercing, she asked questions about the extent to which I was following the Gospel in my life. I admire the woman, she has done a great deal of good for the rural poor and has many good insights about the Christian life. When we parted, I felt a little angry and more than a little guilty about the disparity between the Gospel precepts and my own actions.

Still, I find I have mixed feelings about the value of such prophetic witness. I have other friends who follow the Catholic Worker movement as well. Still other friends are Quakers. These people try to live consistent lives. They try to limit their material goods and conserve energy and resources. My friend with whom I had lunch was dressed very poorly. There was a hole in her slacks.

My friend, the prophet, told me that when she first joined the committee she thought perhaps she would quit because she resisted such an elitist group. (Most of the members are academics.) But, she said, she had come to understand the vulnerability of these people. She had come to distinguish between appearance and reality.

I was pleased at this final admission because I feel that it is unfair to romanticize the poor (as my friend certainly does) and demean the middle class. Economic status is not immediately to be correlated with virtue. It is not having goods which is damning us, but attachment to them.

We must recognize the disparity of appearance and reality. We must come to recognize that there is more than one kind of poverty. Material poverty may or may not be accompanied by emotional poverty. If there is family stability and affection, most people can survive material poverty without permanent scars. Often material poverty is a symptom of emotional poverty. It is family breakdown or illness or other events that cause the lack of material goods.

Conversely, many a person who owns a Volvo and

a beautiful home in the suburbs is filled with self doubts and lack of purpose. Often, the acquisition of and attachment to things is compensation for emotional poverty. So, in looking at the trappings of wealth, we must try to discover the person who feels he or she needs such things.

It is a great disservice automatically to condemn the middle class, the bourgeoisie. It is simply not true that poor people are automatically good and middle class people automatically selfish and materialistic. We must stop looking at one another in terms of the things we have or don't have.

I cannot forget my middle class roots. My parents struggled to give their children a decent standard of living. I cannot reject their efforts. While I may want to simplify my life, I doubt I will reach a point where I will be comfortable in ragged clothing. And I will try to refrain from criticizing those who need great wardrobes to give them a sense of worth. Perhaps people who have things are as much in need of ministrations as those who seemingly have nothing.

It has been demonstrated in religious life, for example, as it has often been lived, that a vow of poverty does not necessarily mean poverty of spirit. It is poverty of spirit, whatever one's external situation, that all must strive for.

It should be remembered that poverty and simplicity of externals is a means, not an end in itself. Having fewer things, wanting fewer things, means having fewer distractions in our lives.

Is there any firm answer to the question of material poverty? Certainly we should try to be consistent. If we want to extend the world's resources, we can cut down on our own consumption to benefit others. But, and this is crucial, we should never look back, never look to see what others are doing, never judge them. If we cannot retain kindness and a nonjudgmental stance, it is best not to try to simplify one's life. Kindness above all, is essential.

How should we live? Each Christian must answer

that question in his or her own way. But each Christian should be encouraged to ponder and to answer that question. Where are the sacrifices I can make? Will they be sacrifices of goods, of money, or of time, and convenience.

It is possible for the rich to be virtuous, but it is harder, I think, because the temptations are so great. Maintaining oneself in a sumptuous lifestyle requires a certain amount of pursuit of worldly treasures. And it is attachment to things and not things themselves that becomes the problem. The question is how willing am I to give up these goods, status, fame, titles. Direct pursuit, I think, takes us away from the Kingdom, but all these things, used rightly, can contribute to God's glory and the building of the Kingdom.

In an affluent society, in the western world, with a superabundance of things, choosing is important. While no one can choose for another, we still can ask one another the right questions. Some of these questions might be:

FOOD: Is it healthful? Is it produced by oppressed people? Does its production benefit the country of its origin? Is it produced through a waste of natural resources? How much should I eat?

CLOTHING: Do I really need all these clothes? Do I really need this new item? Do I have things that others really might need?

AUTOMOBILES: What kind of auto is suited to my needs? Does it waste gas? What are my motives for buying it? Is it safe, well-built? Is it produced by people who are oppressed?

HOUSING: How much is it just to spend on housing? Do I really need a home this large, this luxurious?

RECREATION: Is it prudent to spend this much money on recreation? Are there other types of enjoyment less destructive of health and environment I might enjoy?

IN GENERAL: Has acquiring things become a recreation in my life? How might I replace this habit with something more worthwhile?

In short, the Christian should concern himself with poverty, but must recognize that emotional poverty is every bit as devastating as material poverty. Christians should ask themselves some basic questions about things, detachment, and kindness. Attention to things must not get in the way of attention to the one thing necessary.

INSTITUTIONS I

"An institution is the lengthened shadow of a man."

Ralph Waldo Emerson

IN my job as associate editor of a Catholic weekly, I have interviewed hundreds of persons in the past six years. One kind of person impresses me most, the kind of person who triumphs over a particular problem or a difficult situation. In dealing with his or her own situation, the person discovers certain techniques that might work with others. The person creates a structure to meet the needs of others with the same problem. Thus, the person, by "lengthening his or her shadow," creates an institution.

Now, in the chapter on William Carlos Williams, I pointed out Williams' distrust of institutions, or any attempt to deal with people that would force them into a mold, treat them as numbers rather than as individuals.

But, on the other hand, there is no alternative to institutions for dealing with numbers of people. One cannot care for each person on a one-to-one basis. Too many needs would go unmet. Considering the numbers of people with problems, I see no alternative to institutions.

The challenge, however, is to keep institutions renewed, true to the ideals of their founders, able to respond with humanity, to treat people as individuals.

There are many people who can be summoned to give one-on-one care to another. But some people are frustrated by such an approach. They keep thinking of those, like the person in front of them, who are in similar circumstances, and dream of some kind of structure to meet those needs. There is in this kind of person a certain dissatisfaction with things as they are, with a piecemeal approach. These people dream of a better way, and are willing to take the risks of enfleshing the dream. Another

quality which seems to typify such people is energy, a special gift of the Holy Spirit.

The person who dreams, the creative dreamer, may be a bishop who is open to new ideas and thereby summons other dreamers to his diocese. Or it may be a nun who serves as a college chaplain and has to blaze a trail as a woman in a man's role. It may be a priest who works as a chaplain in a veterans' hospital where a number of alcoholics seek treatment, and sets up a refuge for alcoholic veterans. Or it may be a divorced woman with five young children who begins an interfaith group for Christian single people (divorced, widowed, single). Or it could be a woman who was an unwed mother herself who forms a group which helps unwed mothers find support so that their babies might be born.

In my opinion, such acts are true examples of incarnation. These are people who have transformed something bad into a systematic way of achieving something good.

The above examples are people whom I know personally. Most religious orders and congregations, however, grew out of precisely the same kind of vision and daring. St. Francis of Assisi founded the Franciscans in an attempt to serve the true Jesus and the true Gospel. St. Teresa of Avila reformed her order, returning it to the purity of its intentions. Ignatius of Loyola founded the Jesuits in response to a particular need, and St. Dominic founded the Dominicans in response to the needs of his time. Frederick Ozanam founded the St. Vincent de Paul society because of the needs of the poor. A young French girl, Pauline Jaricot, founded the Society for the Propagation of the Faith out of her concern for the missions. Every religious community traces its foundation to a daring visionary who wanted not to meet one need but to create a system, an institution to meet many needs simultaneously.

The fact that people still found institutions is heartening. It means that in spite of the impotency many of us feel, there are still creative dreamers who envision change and organize to bring it about.

No one can impose such an incarnational act on another, though such an act can be elicited and encouraged where the gifts of people are fostered and recognized.

In my own community there are two immensely successful projects, the brainchildren of a Congregational clergyman. One is a food depository which provides emergency food to the poor. The other is a legislative lobby for improving the lot of the poor, a direct outgrowth of the other experience.

One of these activities is social service. The other is social action. Both are structures which meet needs on a continuing basis. Without structure, there is no continuity. And people need structure to meet large needs.

To Live God's Word

Such structures needn't be large or ecumenical in shape. There are undoubtedly hundreds of needs in each community. We need to pay attention, to look and listen, to discover the needs. We need to feel with the people who suffer. We need to have the generosity to spend the time. We need to "screw our courage to the sticking place," take the leap into the cold water. But more than anything, we need to dream of a difference. It could be a stop sign where there is not one, a recreation center for poor children, an area newsletter to bring people together.

In this age of alienation and isolation, people need bridges built between themselves and other people, not just a rope that will allow a person to swing across the ravine.

Institutions are built out of a person's own experiences, his flesh and blood. In current religious jargon, this phenomenon of ministering to others with the same problems is called "peer ministry." It seems logical that the disabled can help the disabled; the married, the married; the single, the single; and the divorced, divorced people. Essential to any such effort is dreaming of a difference and the willingness to make lemonade out of one's lemons.

INSTITUTIONS II

"A dialectic is any arbitrary system which, since all systems are mere inventions, is necessarily in each case a false premise upon which a closed system is built, shutting those who confine themselves in it from the rest of the world."
William Carlos Williams
The Autobiography of William Carlos Williams

HAVING noted in an earlier chapter that we need institutions (structures) in order to meet people's needs on a larger than one-to-one scale, it is important to reflect on the dangers of institutions as well.

Williams resisted institutions and systems because he thought they lied. They tamed reality, they lacked spontaneity, they failed to deal with people in their uniqueness.

Alas, this seems true of most institutions. Anyone

who has ever had to wait in an emergency room knows what it is to be treated as a thing, simply because efficiency demands that cases be handled as quickly and unemotionally as possible. In other kinds of institutions there is a total resistance to change. They continue in useless modes of activity because "we've always done it this way."

The Church, though to some extent it shares the problems of other institutions, is also, to some extent, an exception. Undoubtedly because the Spirit of God periodically descends to straighten things out (e.g. Vatican II). The Church is always, as Garry Wills said, dying from the top down and being resurrected from the bottom up.

In the post-Vatican II Church, we have struggled to make concrete the impulses of the Spirit. The teaching of Vatican II about co-responsibility, for example, has been enfleshed in the concept of diocesan and parish councils. The great danger, however, is to suppose that these rickety structures will

become sanctified and that the laity will be unable to distinguish substance and form.

Mao Tse Tung was correct, I think, in speaking of the need for perpetual revolution. It is the only way to avoid the petrification of structures and the stultification of members.

Institutions, sytems, structures, especially Christian ones, I believe, should have an "ad hoc" orientation. They should be kept firmly focused on the goal, and when the goal is reached, should be disbanded.

I know of an instance in a nearby parish in which a ladies group disbanded. The decision was a conscious one, made by the full membership, and not simply the effect of declining attendance. The group decided that its orientation was inappropriate in the Post Vatican II Church and wanted to free its members to serve elsewhere.

What a perfect model, I thought, for institutions and systems. Instead of becoming primarily concerned with their own maintenance, they decided to dissolve. What a Christlike gesture!

Structures, like people, should have a life of their own. They are born, reach maturity, and die. And they should not be self-centered, should lay down their lives for others.

Institutions, structures, systems, 1) are necessary for the long-term, large-scale meeting of needs; 2) and are dangerous because they tend to make rigid and permanent what should be fluid and temporary.

Institutions then, in the Christian scheme of things, must see constant reflection and renewal as imperative, and must have Christ as their model.

Part IV

SUFFERING

AFFLICTION

"Extreme affliction, which means physical pain, distress of soul, and social degradation all at the same time, is a nail whose point is applied at the very center of the soul, whose head is all necessity spreading throughout space and time. Affliction is a marvel of divine technique. It is a simple and ingenious device which introduces into the soul of a finite creature the immensity of force, blind, brutal and cold. The infinite distance separating God from the creature is entirely concentrated into one point to pierce the soul at its center."

Simone Weil
"The Love of God and Affliction"
Waiting for God

IN the essay quoted from above, Simone Weil does not end on this despairing note. She points out that a person in such pain can continue to want to love, and indeed, if the soul turns toward God, the sufferer, "finds himself nailed in the very center of the universe." She adds, "In this marvelous dimension, the soul, without leaving the place and the instant where the body to which it is united is situated, can cross the totality of space and time and come into the very presence of God. It is at the intersection of creation and Creator. This point of intersection is the point of intersection of the arms of the cross."

Only a person who had Simone Weil's kind of crucifying suffering perhaps can write of it so articulately. (She died at the age of 34 of tuberculosis after a lifetime of blinding headaches.)

Suffering is perhaps the dimension of incarnation that is most difficult to comprehend or accept. But it is inevitable. The approach of age brings with it inevitable diminishments, limitations. One begins to feel a heaviness in the body, the weight of mortality. As our physical experience of the world changes, so does our experience of past and future. We remember more and anticipate less. There is a young adult generation behind, and an aged generation ahead.

Incarnation requires the graceful acceptance of all these diminishments. Those who are not willing to let go find themselves clinging pathetically to illusions. The small diminishments are all preparations for the ultimate diminishment, death, when we are translated into another realm of being.

Youth and health put matter, the physical, at the service of the spirit. Our bodies, when healthy, are vehicles of our being. When they decline, they are prisons, encumbrances.

One's own diminishments, responded to in openness to the will of God, produce compassion. Confronting one's own mortality means a new way of looking at the rest of humanity, others each living their little lives, signifying what?

In his book *Man's Search for Meaning*, psychiatrist Viktor Frankl writes of his own discoveries after having survived a Nazi concentration camp. Dr. Frankl explores the ways one can find meaning in his or her life: According to logotherapy (the psychiatric technique Dr. Frankl invented) we can discover meaning in life in three different ways: 1) by doing a deed; 2) by experiencing a value; and 3) by suffering.

In elaborating the notion of meaning through suffering, Dr. Frankl says, "Whenever one is confronted with an inescapable, unavoidable situation . . . just then is one given a last chance to actualize the highest value, to fulfill the deepest meaning, the meaning of suffering. For what matters after all is the attitude in which we take our own suffering upon ourselves."

Those last words are particularly significant. The same point is made in Albert Camus' "The Myth of Sisyphus," in which Sisyphus has been condemned endlessly to push a rock up a mountain only to have it roll down again. Sisyphus takes on his suffering, though, accepts the struggle as a challenge, and becomes heroic through the acceptance of his vocation.

There are some, like Sisyphus, for whom suffering is a calling. They are the disabled, the chronically ill, the oppressed. While most of us feel the limitations and oppressions at some point in our lives, those whose vocation it is to suffer may have their whole lives circumscribed by pain. This is not to say that they cannot be happy, but that somehow, their pain must be woven into the fabric of the meaning of their lives.

There is no truer incarnation than carrying the cross throughout one's life, and while mental, and emotional suffering are real, it is Simone Weil's contention that it is physical suffering that is the ultimate degradation. Physical suffering weighs down the soul, drains energy, limits the scope of one's life to that defined by pain.

A life of suffering can become heroically saintly if

the suffering person allows the Lord full rein in his or her illness, allows him or herself to be a victim, cooperates, without ceasing to hate the pain itself, in this co-redemptive act.

The acceptance of suffering and its redemptive power have always been key elements in the Gospel. We usually deny the centrality of the cross. We usually fail also to grasp the sacramental dimension of our daily lives. We need to be reminded and to remind one another of the inherent value of suffering, at the same time praying continually for release and healing.

It is possible both to accept suffering as the Lord's will while at the same time asking for healing. The Lord wills his people to be healthy even though he allows suffering for his own purposes. It is a terrible temptation to accept suffering, to embrace suffering for its own sake, to become accomplices, as Simone Weil said, in our suffering.

A theology of suffering needs to be made quite

explicit in the life of every Christian so that he or she has a reference point. As Dr. Frankl (a Jewish existentialist) points out: "In accepting the challenge to suffer bravely, life has a meaning up to the last moment, and it retains the meaning literally to the end. In other words, life's meaning is an unconditional one, for it includes the potential meaning of suffering."

Sometimes I think partially disabled people suffer more than those who are totally disabled. With total disability, one becomes so completely dependent on the good will of others, aware that one's whole life becomes circumscribed by suffering. It is as though one can give his or her whole life over to the vocation. One is released in such situations from other duties to fulfill the higher calling of creative suffering.

For most people, however, a constant amount of pain or discomfort is not disabling, but simply wears down the energy required to fulfill other tasks:

putting in a full day's work, raising a family. Such persons carry a double burden, coping with the fulfillment of their primary vocation and that of suffering as well. Anyone who has lived with chronic pain understands that it robs one of the virtue of hope. One must achieve in spite of loss of hope.

Dealing creatively with suffering is difficult. For one thing, it is hard to reach the degree of concentration necessary for reflection. In real pain, one feels degraded, abandoned. Without an act of utter trust in the Lord, one is tempted to give up.

In addition to a system of meaning, which explains suffering to the sufferer, there is an equally strong need for a system of support. Whether the suffering is immediate, in one's own body, or proximate, as in that of a parent of a disabled child, there is a need for a community of support and comfort. Aloneness is perhaps the ultimate desolation that physical suffering leads to.

Providing this system of support is the vocation of

all Christians. Binding up others' wounds should be everyone's priority, or at least offering a hand to hold. We must reach a point where we see Christ in every sufferer. Sharing our belief (our system of meaning) is secondary to providing that support. Meeting physical needs is always the priority. That is why evangelization, preaching the word, is the handmaid to charity and not the other way around. Simone Weil put it well: "Here below, physical pain, and that alone, has the power to chain down our thoughts."

The system of support means helping the person live in the present as much as possible since hope, in Eliot's words "would be hope for the wrong thing." It also means helping the sufferer to surrender to the stream of life, not giving up, but letting go. There must be the willingness to look for beauty, to perceive every day as a gift.

There must ultimately be, in the sufferer, a sense

of instrumentality, of cooperation in some obscure divine plan. But the sheer weight of suffering impedes this kind of abandonment. It is by having others help him with his burden that a person becomes capable of responding to grace, of trusting completely in the Lord.

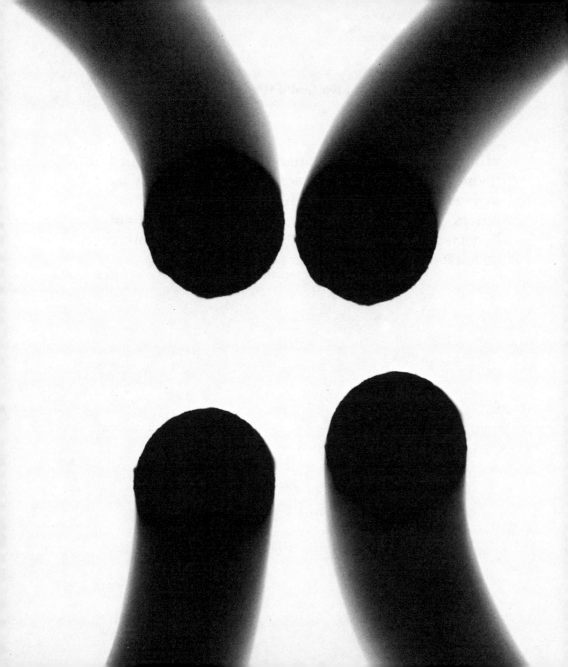

HEALING

"That evening they brought him many who were possessed by devils. He cast out the spirits with a word and cured all who were sick. This was to fulfill the prophecy of Isaiah: 'He took our sicknesses away and carried our diseases for us."

Matthew 8:16-17

HEALING is a sacramental act. Whether through nature, through the intervention of a physician, through the administration of the sacrament of healing, or by use of the gift of healing, the making of a sick body well is a holy act.

Perhaps in no other act than the restoration of health does the feeling of gratitude manifest itself so strongly. And perhaps no other act can manifest the wonder that is health, that we take so for granted as the substratum of all other acts. It is no wonder that

Yvonne Goulet

healing was a key element of the ministry of Jesus. Healing demonstrates his lordship. Even the seas and the microbes are subject to him. Even the lame can walk through his power.

If illness demonstrates that the material world is subject to the effects of sin, a restoration of health recalls that God wants good things for us. Nowhere is affliction considered to be a good thing.

But in the modern dissociation of body and mind, the body came to be the province of the medical world, which promptly lost its faith, and the spirit became the province of the Church, which promptly forgot the body.

One therefore finds healers who are nothing more than technicians offering their technical abilities for a fee, having no sense of the sacredness of life, of the totality of personhood, or the transcendent value of their calling. Little wonder their operations may succeed while the patient dies.

One also finds that the spiritual is too little called

upon in the area of healing. It is as though Jesus, in his healing ministry, was only behaving as a magician and not leaving a heritage of healing power available to his ministers. Why, for example, did the Sacrament of the Sick become transformed into the Sacrament of the Dying? Although there is now an attempt to recover the healing power of this sacrament, it tends nevertheless to be reserved for those who are elderly or seriously ill. The sacrament should, I think, be made available to all who experience diminishments, whether short-term or long-term, whether life-threatening or simply annoying.

The sacraments are essentially signs of the healing grace of God which continues to be available to people. They are not the exclusive conveyors of that grace. God does not ration grace through the Sacraments.

I think the Church should use its healing power liberally rather than sparingly. Why not commission or "ordain" those who have the gift of healing?

If the body played a more central part in our spirituality, the opening up to the healing power of God in sacraments would be clearer. A new consciousness of the body is needed in order to release the Church's power to heal.

But the gift of healing is not exclusively the province of the religious community. There are those who are physicians who have the gift of healing and those who do not. A person must discover whether a physician has a sense of instrumentality, sacramentality in his work, whether the health of the total person is his or her concern, whether he or she is encouraging an unhealthy dependency.

There are two approaches to the treating of disease commonly used in the medical profession: 1) drugs, and 2) surgery. There are, of course, also special diets and exercise regimens that are also recommended, but many physicians seem to rely primarily on chemical or surgical intervention. Drugs often deal with symptoms and not causes.

Surgery often causes as many problems as it solves. This is not to say that drugs and surgery are not blessings, properly administered, but to suggest that the most ancient healing technique, the laying on of hands, has a place in the healing process.

I have recently been healed of a back problem through osteopathic manipulation. Before I found a person who would attempt to look at my problems in terms of posture and balance, the proper alignment of the body, I had three MD's who told me that they could find nothing wrong with my body. (One aide to an orthopedic physician explained that the doctor "only sees one back a day.")

As a result of my back problem, I have changed my concept of such approaches to health as manipulation, massage, acupressure, reflexology, and various other techniques which stimulate the body's own healing power without surgical or chemical intervention.

That the medical establishment will not refer

people with muscular-skeletal problems (that surgery is not suited for) to osteopathic physicians is, I
think, a great scandal. There are undoubtedly persons who have been in pain for years (as I was for
six months) before finding a competent physician
who could treat the problem with the conservative
treatment of adjustment.

There are many other scandals in the medical
establishment—physicians who smoke and give bad
example, those who prescribe various drugs without
any concern for the safety of the user, those who
will operate and remove a healthy organ as a
preventive measure.

With new breakthroughs in biology which have
created the possibilities of genetic manipulation,
test tube babies, and other anomalies, the inability
of the medical establishment to deal with ethical
questions becomes more and more apparent. There
is the posture that information about a "defective"
fetus can be handed on to a person in a value-free

environment. The very notion that it is the role of a healer to perform a non-therapeutic abortion is, I think, frightening.

But the religious community has been equally guilty of creating the gap between medicine and religion. The Church makes pronouncements about theoretical questions, but seldom comes to terms with people in concrete circumstances. A continuing dialogue between the medical establishment and the Church should take place. There should be more cooperation in dealing with the total person so that those with long-term and catastrophic illness, for example, receive the encouragement of both faith and science.

What religion can give to medical science is a sense of life as a continuum, with death as an integral part of the process. A physician cannot deal appropriately with a dying patient if he or she refuses to take into consideration the inevitability of death. Without some concept of an afterlife, how can a healer incorporate the notion of final illness into his work?

Medicine is one field in which the increasing involvement of women in key roles is having a humanizing effect. Perhaps it is because women are more attuned to the rhythms of nature (in view of their own participation in natural rhythms; that is, women who have not been alienated from their own bodies). Interestingly, it is two women, Doctors Elisabeth Kubler-Ross and Cecily Saunders (founder of the Hospice movement) who have provided the breakthrough which allows the dying patient to be considered as a person first and a patient only secondarily.

Dr. Ross has emphasized the need for the physician or any helping professional to listen to what the patient is saying, and on the non-verbal, symbolic level as well as on the verbal, so that the person can be helped to deal with the fact of his death. Dr. Ross takes a humble stance in the face of the ending of life: that it is the dying patient who can teach us about dying. By acknowledging the dignity of the person and the authenticity and value of his or her experience, Dr. Ross makes the comforting of the dying a holy act. What a contrast to the sad concept of abandoning the dying patient because he cannot be cured.

The healing professions, in my opinion, are far too concerned with the sick and sickness and far too little concerned with health and the healthy. How little health education there is. People know more about their homes and their automobiles than they do about their bodies. (Bodies, ought, perhaps, to come with owners' manuals?)

Although the women's movement has some bizarre emphases, I think the idea (though not the actuality as they depict it) of "controlling one's own body" is a sound one. We ought to be able to do many things to preserve and enhance our health and medicine should help acquaint people with the ways of making themselves healthy rather than ways of "getting them into the system." Much more attention, for example, should be given in schools to lifelong exercise habits, diet, nutrition, the damaging effects of smoking and alcohol. Posture is a terribly important area that should not be overlooked since so many problems that people think are irremediable can be managed with simple adjustment processes.

And what about the insanity of such things as silicone implants and fluoridated water? I know my opposition to the latter concept makes me sound like a neanderthal, but with new findings every day about the damage done to bodies by chemicals once thought safe, I think better ways of preserving dental health should be found. Fluoride 1) tastes terrible, and 2) violates the rights of those opposed to it to drink unadulterated water. And silicone implants (for breast enlargement) it seems to me, whether or not they are dangerous, are built on a false self-concept (no pun intended). A woman who wants her breast size increased should receive counseling rather than plastic surgery.

To summarize, healing should be more natural and less technological. There should be far more attention to health than to disease. Preventive medicine is the key word. There should be more of a sense of the spiritual origins of illness (and more research) and more direct involvement of spiritual ministers in healing. The laying on of hands should be considered a key conservative element in treatment and physicians should be open to information about healing made available from sources such as osteopathy and eastern medicine (acupressure, acupuncture).

Bodies, as we know, are holy. They are meant to be temples and servants of the spirit. When affliction occurs, it is to be remedied if at all possible.

Yvonne Goulet

Health and healings should always be desired. But incarnation will take place only when the Church takes more interest in peoples' bodies, and the medical establishment shows more concern for their souls.

HEALTH

"The first wealth is health.

Ralph Waldo Emerson
"The Conduct of Life"

ONE challenge of incarnation is finding the right emphasis on health, food, and fitness in our lives. Having a body means being responsible for this wonderful gift. Having good health means the responsibility of maintaining and enhancing that health.

A few years ago I wrote an article for a Catholic magazine titled, "It's a Sin to Smoke." My thesis, which I meant quite seriously, is that smoking, which is proved to be harmful to the health of the smoker and to others who breathe the smoke of the cigarette, violates the law of love and its more explicit formulation in the Fifth Commandment. Smoking, I said, violates the law of love by sinning against God, our neighbors, and ourselves. The sin against God is assuming dominion over our bodies when only the Lord has dominion. We are poor stewards when we abuse our health.

We offend ourselves, I pointed out, because we injure our health and impair our efficiency; and we offend others by causing discomfort, and in some cases physical damage to others, born or unborn, by endangering the financial security of those who depend upon the smoker, and by giving bad example to young people.

I was roundly denounced for my position, which reminded many readers of fanaticism. But a letter to the magazine from an anesthesiologist who works daily with patients (who have chronic bronchitis after only ten years of one pack a day), I found heartening. He said: "There is no question that, morally, smoking is a sin, grave sin."

Many of the other responses astounded me. I thought people might be angry, but I also thought

the argument was so sound that at least they would have to see that smoking was a form of self-mutilation.

Apparently, people don't think of moral evil in terms of health matters. But if gluttony and dueling are considered by the Church to be sins because they represent an inversion of a natural appetite, or place the person in unnecessary danger, why can't matters of health and safety be sins, both individual and corporate?

A number of respondents called my article silly. Others rationalized. "Most of life's little pleasures are sooner or later found harmful. Personally, I don't wish to live to be 95 anyway." "It seems to me that should we agree with Ms. Goulet, we might in the near future be confronted with the question, "Is it a sin to eat eggs?' " Others were more thoughtful, suggesting that a categorical denunciation of an act is no longer acceptable: "The real sin depends not so much on the action itself as the state of the conscience of the individual who performs those actions." Some even quoted Scripture: "Matt. 15:11. It is not what goes into a man's mouth that makes him impure; it is what comes out of his mouth."

I was intrigued with the number of respondents who apparently see no connection between stewardship of one's body and moral responsibility. Many of these, apparently, were priests. One man said he had confessed excessive smoking to three different priests and none would look on the act as sinful.

And many people refuse to consider sinful a matter on which they simply have failed to 1) form their consciences, and 2) explore the moral implications.

While I think smoking is the most vivid example of a poor health habit that can be sinful (because it violates, in a direct way, the law of love), I do think that people have a responsibility, now that we have the information to make better choices about how we will live, to avoid things that are harmful and care for the body that God gives each of us.

I don't want to sound judgmental and I, of course, am making a distinction between something that is sinful in the objective order but may or may not be sinful in the subjective circumstances of a given person. And I understand that Jesus was far more concerned with people following the law of love than anything else. He knew we had human faults and failings, and he made no hard dietary rules.

It is not because of any Church rule or explicit teaching of Jesus that I think preserving one's health is important, but because the body and spirit are one. The body is the vehicle whereby we are present in the world and through which the Spirit of God works. I am limited in my communication with the world by my body. My body is very important.

The need for a theology of the body, I think, becomes more obvious every day. Unless we have essentials in essential positions in our lives, we tend to expand the importance of less critical matters. For many of those who have no faith, however, accidentals become essentials. For example there are those who make of food a faith in itself and ask truths of the health food salesman as if he were a priest or a guru.

On the other hand, there are very few people who are consistent in their beliefs and action who care about world hunger enough not to waste food; who care about the environment enough to conserve energy.

I am really opposed, personally, to the killing of animals, and yet I eat meat. I see a possible future as a vegetarian once I understand nutrition enough to pursue the nutritional techniques needed. We are all on a journey toward becoming consistent.

It's quite clear to me, in any case, that many diseases have an origin in the spirit, the psyche. If one is living a life that is not free, in which one is frustrated and unhappy, diseases can invade. Many diseases are caused by improper nutrition or over-eating.

And lack of exercise itself can bring on disease. I am always amazed by the number of committed Christians for whom care of the body is unimportant. I know many priests, for example, who smoke and drink to excess. I know many religious women for whom exercise is simply non-existent, and yet who are preoccupied with disease and disability.

How many elderly people cannot move easily because they simply stopped moving at a young age and their muscles have become fixed in a given position? How many diseases of joints and muscles come simply from lack of use, as a hinge grows rusty?

Perhaps it might be said that such misuse of the body is a disease, like alcoholism. If so, why aren't people on both sides of the dichotomy, body and spirit, working to mend the split?

As indicated before the process of yoga takes into

consideration such matters as proper exercise, flexibility, breathing, which dispose the person to meditation. Eastern spirituality seems to know that the spirit is grounded in the physical.

I was pleased to learn that some Christians pay attention to fitness and not just in the concept of the "Christian athlete." At Oral Roberts University in Oklahoma, fitness is required. Not only must students and faculty members maintain a given weight, but buildings are purposely built far apart to require walking.

In many colleges and universities, the aim of sports programs is learning exercises and developing health habits that will last a lifetime. A person can't play basketball forever, but he or she can always dance, or golf, or bicycle.

Contrast this approach to the fitness of the person with those of schools were the only real athletic concern is the football team. What a temporary and limited view of the body.

Yvonne Goulet

The point of all this is that physical well-being is important because our bodies are gifts. We are responsible for them. Our stewardship of the material world begins and ends with our own bodies, which should be respected, and cared for lovingly. A sound spirit in a sound body is still a good idea.

Part V

BECOMING

Yvonne Goulet

REALITY

"Reality is often grim and terrible on its surface; it's almost always grim and terrible underneath and until one penetrates to its innermost core. At its innermost core, reality is infinitely tender; infinitely strong to sustain, to console, even permanently to delight and enrapture the heart of man. Only heroism can penetrate to the innermost core of reality—only heroism fused with humility."

Russel Wilbur
"The Quintessence of Catholicism"

IT seems quite obvious to ask, in a book about incarnation, what is it that is being incarnated. What is the presence that is coming to be in my flesh and in the material world? Essential to a fuller understanding of and participation in incarnation is a sense of the infinite gentleness, lovableness, vulnerability of the God who loves us.

Theologian Monika Hellwig said that the amazing thing is not that Jesus is like God, but that God is like Jesus. If God is like Jesus, he depends on people, can be lonely, cares about individual human beings, can be hurt.

We must change our concepts of God from almighty, all-knowing, (which are no doubt true) to the heart of his reality. God is love. Love is utter self-emptying, utter self-giving.

In being made in God's image, we are made with the possibility for infinite self-emptying, infinite lovableness, gentleness, vulnerability. Finding our true selves means the peeling away of appearances, of the layers we tend to accrue and finding the lovable image of God in all its freshness.

Yvonne Goulet

The separation between us and God is the great fiction. Where there is love, there is no separation. We have already entered the Kingdom. We have already begun eternity. All that is truly left for us is to see the wonder of the reality that is ours.

Of course, there is suffering: that is because there is sin. But it is not that God stands outside human suffering, that he allows human beings to be tortured. It is rather that human suffering is a privilege of humanity, to participate in the sufferings of Christ.

God is not outside ourselves and our experiences. He is with us. He is within us. That is the meaning of incarnation, a greater understanding and appreciation of this mystical vision.

And yet, as Teilhard has said, union differentiates. By being united with God, we are not absorbed, our identity is not destroyed. We are affirmed in our personhood precisely by the fact of

union, precisely by the opening up to the power of God.

Thomas Merton is quoted by Ron Seitz in an article in *U.S. Catholic* (December, 1978) to the effect that one enters the monastery "to heal the illusion of separation, the separation of you from your true person, from the world in creation, and especially from God." One "goes home in redemption," Merton says, "by curing the inner split between you and God the incarnate creator, what we sometimes call in Mystical Theology original sin."

One of the most profound treatments of the concept of sin as separation is that of Robert Penn Warren in his novel *All the King's Men.*

The interpretation of the novel with which I most concur is that which says the book is about original sin. In commenting on the theme of the novel, James Ruoff notes the characters' coming to terms with

moral decisions but that with all human beings they
are unable to see the effect of their decisions:
"Ironically, the Fall simultaneously gave man moral
vision (i.e. the knowledge of good and evil) and
struck him blind; it gave him immediate, *a priori*
knowledge of good and evil as it related to any moral
decision but it left him blind to the ultimate purpose
or direction or consequences of the fact. As an individual, he is master of his soul in a moment of crucial moral decision; as a species, he is a pawn in a
cosmic game, the ultimate meaning or purpose of
which he can never know."

It is healing the effects of this split that faith and
prayer can achieve for the individual human being.
By perceiving the original goodness, the Christian,
the believer, can live so that others will begin to see
the glimmer of meaning and wholeness as well.

Close to the end of the Warren novel there is a
passage dictated by Ellis Burden, whom the pro-

tagonist, Jack Burden, assumes is his father. It functions as a sort of chorus, relating the activities of the plot to Warren's theme:

> The creation of man whom God in his fore-
> knowledge knew doomed to sin was an awful
> index of God's omnipotence. For it would have
> been a thing of trifling and contemptible ease
> for perfection to create more perfection. To do
> so would be to speak truth, be not creation,
> but extension. Separateness is identity and the
> only way for God to create, truly create, man
> was to make him separate from God himself and
> to be separate from God is to be sinful. The
> creation of evil is therefore the index of God's
> glory and his power. That had to be so that the
> creation of good might be the index of man's
> glory and power. But by God's help. By his help
> in his wisdom.

To Live God's Word

The vision of Ellis Burden in this passage is the view of the surface of reality, or of reality as far as one can penetrate without grace and faith and prayer. As far as one can penetrate there is only sin and separation, grief and grimness. But with the eyes of faith and grace, the childlike eyes of a saint, of a Thomas Merton, the separation is seen to be fictive. The only way to reach this vision is by changing the self to become as little and lovable and humble as the reality that is to be perceived.

Original sin and its effects of evil—moral and physical—is very much with us, but beyond that is original goodness, which was never extinguished, only clouded by our failure of vision. Not only is original goodness present, but it is a person, it loves us, and it wants the triumph of good. The very failure of vision is itself the effect of sin, as the previous passage tells us.

So it is not that things are separate and terrible. It

is just that we cannot see things as they really are. Ultimately it is not knowledge that reveals the truth, but love.

Russell Wilbur, in the essay quoted in the epigraph at the beginning of this chapter, speaks of the need for heroism and humility. He points out that the heroism he speaks of is not that heroism which is audacious. (What Gandhi would call, "standing behind the cannon") but the kind which is enduring, which by God's grace accepts the ills that happen. True heroism is the patient, trusting gesture of letting the Lord do his will in us.

Wilbur's notion of heroism is one that goes beyond what he calls "personal humility." Although he calls personal humility indispensable, he said that much more necessary is "human humility" by which he means a sense of the place of the species of man in the universe, the notion of our contingency.

And those who suffer, Wilbur says, find within

themselves "a mysterious presence, one who comes to suffer in them, with them, and for them."

We must change our concept of a God out there, far beyond and far above human experience to a God who is identified more with the little people than the great. Like Jesus, God loves the poor, the powerless, the humble, the meek, the merciful. God himself is like that, humble, meek, little, merciful, pure. And we have the possibility of recovering our own original purity which lives beneath the accretions of the world.

In discovering how lovable God is, we discover how lovable each of us is.

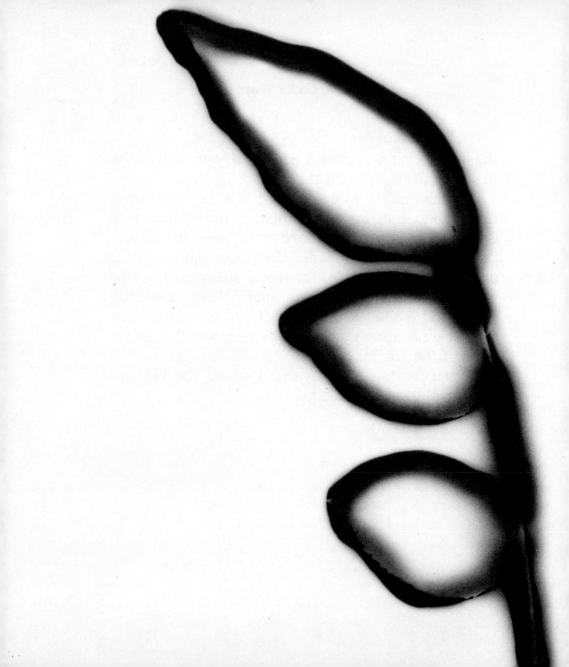

TRUST

> "See, either we are one with the Holy Spirit or
> not, eh? And if the Incarnation, the Word made
> flesh, is a living reality then the whole cosmos is
> sacramentalized, is redeemed, is sacred and
> holy. Is really Church, see (laughing) and you
> can't get out and can't escape that even if you
> wanted to."
>
> Thomas Merton
> quoted by Ron Seitz

SAINTS, it is said, are joyous. The reason is that
they know something the rest of us don't know, or at
least perceive something the rest of us don't
perceive. The last chapter dealt briefly with the vision that allows the person to penetrate the multiplicity of the world and see the one that holds things
together. Similarly, that kind of vision allows a
person to penetrate the appearance of things and
touch their reality.

Yvonne Goulet

All of us break through to that vision, it seems, at some time in our lives. It may be when we are in love, or at the birth of a baby, or when we travel, or when we see scenes of incredible beauty. It may be when we are praying. We suddenly are flooded with the experience (not just the belief) that "all will be well and all manner of things shall be well."

My own experience of the reality of God came about 11 years ago when I was on a tour of Great Britain. This particular day, a friend and I took a bus tour of the Lake Country of England. It was not just that the country is wild and lovely, but that it seemed permeated with an adorable presence. The feeling lasted for the full time the tour lasted, about eight hours. I've never had quite such an experience again.

But experience of the world's order and beauty is not the usual way of things. We are meant to live by faith and hope, in love. We are meant to treasure and remember these peak experiences so that they can ligthen our burdens and our dark nights of the soul.

We are meant to live in trust of this lovable being who created us in his own image, who knows us more intimately than we know ourselves. We are meant to trust the person who lives in us, and works through us to the extent we ask him to.

Trust is very intimately linked with the notion of taking reality in small portions, not making ourselves grand plans and great schemes, not responding to the reality we find ourselves in. One of the things we have to trust in is that we will be given not only the situation but all the tools with which to deal with it gracefully.

Trust means saying no to yearning for things other than they are. Rather, it is the attention to the present moment and present circmstances in which God is talking to us.

Yvonne Goulet

While it could promote a kind of smugness to say that God loves us as we are, that is still true. I often feel that God loves me even more when I have not been particularly saintly. He is quite aware of our limitations and much more forgiving than we dare to hope.

The trouble with those of us who reached adulthood in the pre-Vatican II period is that we still cannot comprehend that God is a lover, and not a policeman. And we cannot believe that life and salvation are about liberation and not judgment.

Elisabeth Kubler-Ross described the experience at the Nazi concentration camp that led her to her work with death and dying. In the light of what she has learned from peoples' after-life experiences, she maintains that there is a judgment immediately after death in which one does review the results, both good and bad, of his choices. Although Hitler would have to review all the pain that he caused others, she said he would also be able to know the good results that occurred, that, for example, all the work with death and dying that is an indirect outcome of his influence.

Life is often grim, and we are meant to live responsibly. But the joy should break through.

This morning I was driving to work, feeling rather down at the prospect of teaching an early morning class, when I saw the sun's rays glinting off the church tower and a flock of seagulls rising into the sky beyond. The scene was so lovely I was distracted, and the moment caused joy to break through my sullen attitude.

These moments are like gifts I think, which must be savored.

One of my most delightful recent discoveries is that there is a group of people called "The World Saunter Society." The movement, which claims some 6000 members worldwide, was created according to a UPI report, "during a front porch debate among faculty members of Lake Superior State College a few years ago."

The group is dedicated "to the preservation, in today's jet age, mechanized society, of such frivolous pursuits as the impromptu stroll through the garden."

As an inveterate saunterer, I find sauntering to be a wonderful metaphor for the Christian's pilgrimage. Life should be much more like a saunter than a jog.

Saunterers are interested in their ultimate goal, eternal life, but they are in no particular hurry to get there. They are far more concerned with the now, with today, with the adventure of living. They take as much pleasure in the means as in the end. The ride to work in the morning can be a beautiful experience.

A saunterer enjoys life. He is always willing to go along with a spontaneous adventure. A true saunterer never loses the ability to wonder at the world.

There is a Zen Buddhist axiom to "Do what you are doing," not to divide your mind, to give one's whole self to a pursuit.

Notice the joy, the vitality of Thomas Merton's remark. A hermit, he was totally involved in the world. In spite of life's pain, the saunterer never loses the ability to enjoy.

Listen to Merton: "See, either we are with the Holy Spirit or not." Consider the utter logic of it. If God is with us, who can be against us? Why should we be afraid? Or if he is not, then the whole structure of our faith is a sham. The initial faith makes possible the trust. And the trust makes possible the joy.

The saunterer (i.e. the Christian pilgrim) is one who says yes to God, yes to creation and its beauty. Yes to life. Yes to faith. Yes to God's will as it is manifested in events.

It is not the absence of suffering that causes the

Yvonne Goulet

joy. It is the ability to put all things into perspective, not to give matters more than the proper amount of attention, to remember, in the midst of all distractions, the one thing necessary.

Believers, I think, have fun because the very human situation itself is incongruous. It begins with belief. Belief brings trust, and trust brings joy.

TIME

"There is one fundamental theme which I have wishes to emphasize throughout these studies: the centrality of the finite concrete as the only healthy and effective path to whatever has traditionally been regarded as the goal of the human being, or for that matter, of the total human personality. It does not matter whether we call that the infinite or peace or insight or maturity."

William F. Lynch, S.J.
. . *Christ and Apollo*

IN developing this idea, Father Lynch adds that "another way of describing our situation is to say that the imagination, to get anywhere, must course through the actual phases or stages or mysteries of the life of man."

The notion of time in incarnation is a central theme of Father Lynch's book.

To Live God's Word

According to Father Lynch, the passage through various phases produces moments of insight and illumination which are necessary to and help create the next point of insight. But the rejection of this movement through time is costly. The attempt to hold on to any one time, such as adolescence, is detrimental to a person. It prevents the surrender to the next stage and the next level of growth.

This process of insight seems to be accelerated in those people who are disabled or diseased. The insights that are necessary for the illumination of one's situation seem to come at the age when they are required. For example, one parent of a disabled child told me that a four-year-old who has suffered is as wise as an old person.

Another form of rejection of time, Father Lynch points out, is to escape from the real world into fantasy or into the life of the mind, whereas all wisdom comes through contact with the finite and the temporal.

Yvonne Goulet

Time is not something outside, Father Lynch tells us: it is within our bodies. As such it is nothing foreign. As we age, there seems to be more awareness of the body, which is subject to the vicissitudes of matter. I have become aware, for example, of a new distinction between myself and my body. I inhabit my body but it is not me. Its separateness makes it quite clear that I shall not need it for eternal life.

Along with a new awareness of the limitations of matter, time brings a sense of the need to live more deliberately. Certainly one can't live a totally planned life. There must be room for the spontaneous. But one's life ought to have some sort of plan, some sort of direction, more steering than drifting. There should be a sort of hunger for experience, for excellence, in one's life.

There should be as much desire for creative leisure, however, as for achievement. Wasting time should be allowed for.

Everyone, in addition to longing for eternal life, seems to hunger for some kind of earthly immortality as well. The most obvious way to have a monument is to have children. They are the promise of further life.

For a person who has no children, there is a kind of mourning the lost ones never born.

For such persons, living in the concrete means accepting this fact and redirecting that "parental energy" into the needs that are clear and present.

Whether or not one has children, one reaches a point where, with a new generation growing to maturity, one assumes a parental role. One suddenly perceives that more people are now younger than he or she is than older, and the weight of responsibility toward both the younger and older generations becomes more obvious. This may be even more true of those who do not have children than it is of those who do.

This is not to say that one assumes a parental role

all the time (we play various roles) but that there is a sense of stewardship of the world, a commitment to the future in younger people. The young are, as Arthur Miller says in his play, "All My Sons" and all my daughters. Unless a person goes beyond the ties of blood and recognizes those of spirit, he or she will never be the person who might be. But these ties of spirit extend to the past as well as the future. In *All the King's Men*, protagonist Jack Burden comes very late to discovery of the identity of his true father, but he comes to a greater recognition: "(Does he think I am his son? I cannot be sure. Nor can I feel that it matters, for each of us is the son of a million fathers.)"

Incarnation, I think, means recognizing that the physical act of giving birth and of nurturing are not the determinants of responsibility. Everyone who comes within my sphere is my brother and mother and child. Instead of mourning lost possibilities, it is necessary to do what I can, where I am, with what I have.

The most dangerous words for a true incarnation are "It might have been." Post Mortems are a terrible waste of time and energy. Living in the present is true wisdom.

The surrender to time, I think, is to accept each moment as a gift, each with its own uniqueness and irreplaceability in our lives. Wisdom is in traveling light, in giving away, in not trying to hold on, in embracing each new experience and stage with passion.

Although it is natural to mourn losses, there is actually nothing in our experience that is ever lost. As Viktor Frankl says in *Man's Search for Meaning,* there is a positive way to look at life: The person who attacks the problems of life actively, he says, "is like the man who removes each successive leaf from his calendar and files it neatly and carefully away after having jotted down a few diary notes on the back. He can reflect with pride and joy on all the richness set down in these notes, on all the life he has already lived to the full. What will it matter to him if he notices he is growing old." Instead of envying the young, such a person, Dr. Frankl says, could say to himself: "No thank you. Instead of possibilities, I have realities in my past, not only the reality of work done and of love loved, but of suffering suffered." In a sense, a person who has lived thusly can look at time as his monument.

Nothing is more pathetic than the attempt to hold onto the past. That does not mean that people shouldn't stay vital and interested in activities, but it is a recognition that youth consists more in flexibility of outlook and enthusiasm than physical appearances. A certain gracious obeisance to the laws of nature is required. And this surrender brings its own wisdom, its own happiness.

American society is devastating, I think, with its

view of aging. Thirty is considered antique. The Europeans, it seems to me, have a far healthier viewpoint, with a recognition of the values of maturity.

If detachment is a principal quality of a life of incarnation, then detachment from one's earlier self is an inherent part of growth.

The surrender to time allows us to look back without regret as it allows us to look ahead with hope. The past is never static, we learn. It is alive because it lives in us. Because we live with effects, bad and good, of earlier decisions, past events always have new meanings, new effects, new dimensions.

I find that growing older gives me a greater appreciation of older people. They deserve honor simply for lasting. They are the survivors in the battle with experience that so many lose. They have withstood myriad pressures and still can care for events and meanings and relationships. It is older

Yvonne Goulet

people who have aged gracefully who can help us all through our individual "passages."

It is far more important for the human being to conquer time than to conquer space. It is far more important to understand what one experiences than go in reckless quest of new experiences. It is not in coming to know everything that we truly incarnate the Lord, but in coming to know ourselves very well.

Epilogue

LIVING THE WORD

"We should not search for an abstract meaning in life. Everyone has his own specific vocation or mission in life; everyone must carry out a concrete assignment that demands fulfillment."

Victor Frankl
Man's Search for Meaning

LIVING the Word, I think, means recognizing that one is truly irreplaceable. Recently there was a remake of a 1940s movie (the earlier version starred Jimmy Stewart, the remake Marlo Thomas) about a person who wished he'd never been born. He was shown, through supernatural intervention, what the lives of people would have been like had he never lived. He became grateful when enlightened by the awareness of all he had been to others in his brief span on earth.

Yvonne Goulet

Each of us is unique, with gifts, abilities, tasks, yes, even a mission that no one can do for us. And Frankl is very wise in saying that we discover that mission not in some abstract way, by finding a vocation, or a profession. We discover our unique vocation by the events and people and circumstances of our lives. That is what incarnation means, that God is speaking continually to us, living continually in us, acting continually through us.

As incarnation means the recognition of our own uniqueness, so it means seeing the uniqueness in every person. In terms of my living the Gospel, it means that there are people for whom Christ can only exist in me. If I refuse to be his instrument, the coming of the Kingdom is delayed, and sin and sadness are strengthened.

Finding our mission means responding to life afresh as its meaning is manifested to us. It means being flexible, able to change directions, and letting

other dimensions of our personalities emerge if certain options are foreclosed.

Looking at our life from the point of view of the afterlife is a common technique by which to get people to focus on what is truly important in their lives. In Thornton Wilder's play *Our Town*, we have a view of Grovers Corners, New Hampshire, from the point of view of a girl who has died. The play has a special quality, concerning, as it does, lost opportunities. It presents life as it might have been lived.

This technique might be called viewing things "sub specie aeternitatis." While it is useless to dwell on past matters that cannot be remedied, it is highly useful to look at our present circumstances from the point of view of how we would see things to be at our deaths. So valid is this technique that Victor Frankl has made it the categorical imperative of logotherapy: "So live as if you were already living for the second time and as if you had acted the first time as wrongly as you are about to act now."

To Live God's Word

The technique is also used in career counseling, as people are asked to write their own obituaries, detailing their accomplishments. Asking a person to look at the present as past gives him the opportunity to make choices which will allow him to fulfill what he perceives as his most basic needs.

Elisabeth Kubler-Ross from her research indicates that there is something after death similar to a particular judgment, in which a person reviews his life and sees the good and bad effects of his actions. She also speaks of asking one 85-year-old woman how she would change things if she had her life to live over. She said the woman replied that she would "relax more, dance more, make more mistakes, take more trips, have more real problems and fewer imaginary ones, eat more ice cream and fewer beans, forget my raincoat and parachute and travel light, ride more merry-go-rounds and pick more daisies."

Our temptation is so often security. I think it is

Yvonne Goulet

quest for security that so often keeps us from living life to the full. We carry our raincoat and umbrella, we anticipate the worst and double our problems thereby.

One problem in living is that we think so often of ends and not of means. By focusing on the ends, we often compromise, taking short cuts to get where we want to be. However, if we can look at all persons, events, and situations not in terms of what or where they will take us, but in terms of themselves, we would purify our motives.

Living the Word means not being afraid of living sequentially. It is a quest for the fullness of life.

Living the Word means accepting every day as a challenge. It means taking the risks necessary to enflesh the Gospel even when or perhaps especially when it is most difficult. It means making choices that will bring a little more care and beauty into the world. Living the Word means letting the Word live in us.